Selections

from

THE BOOK OF
COMMON PRAYER

THE BOOK OF COMMON PRAYER (2019)

Also available from Anglican Liturgy Press

THE BOOK OF COMMON PRAYER (2019) Pew Edition
ISBN 978-1-7334727-7-7

THE BOOK OF COMMON PRAYER (2019) Deluxe Edition - Leather
ISBN 978-1-7334727-1-5

THE BOOK OF COMMON PRAYER (2019) Deluxe Edition – Leatherette
ISBN 978-1-7323448-4-6

THE BOOK OF COMMON PRAYER (2019) Pocket Edition
ISBN 979-8-9878026-7-0

THE BOOK OF COMMON PRAYER (2019) Pocket Edition – Leather
ISBN 979-8-9878026-8-7

anglicanhousepublishers.org

Selections

from

THE BOOK OF COMMON PRAYER

(2019)

for

Personal Use

ANGLICAN LITURGY PRESS

Selections from the Book of Common Prayer (2019) for Personal Use

TABLE *of* CONTENTS

PREFACE

Christianity—the fullness of the good news about Jesus Christ—came very early to what would eventually be called *Anglia* (England) through the witness of soldiers, sailors, merchants, and missionaries. Legend holds that the biblical tomb-giver, Joseph of Arimathea, was among the first of those scattered evangelists.

The early Christian mission in the British Isles was an encounter with pagan tribes and societies. Converts banded together, and in this context communities of common prayer, learning, and Christ-like service emerged, living under agreed rules. Thus "monasteries" became centers of the evangelization of this remote region of the Roman world, and ever more so as the empire disintegrated. Early heroes and heroines leading such communities bore names that are still remembered and celebrated, names like Patrick, Brigid, David, Columba, Cuthbert, and Hilda. Haphazardly, and without a centralized hierarchy or authority, what emerged in Britain, by God's grace, was a Church that saw herself, in each of her local manifestations, as part of the One, Holy, Catholic, and Apostolic Church: culturally attuned and missionally adaptive, but ever committed to and always propagating "the faith that was once for all delivered to the saints" (JUDE 1:3).

Reform came in various waves, based more in the Roman systems of Diocese and parish. At the end of the sixth century, Augustine, a Benedictine monk and first Archbishop of Canterbury, was sent out from Rome by Pope Gregory the Great with instructions that encouraged preservation of local customs when they did not conflict with universal practice. Dunstan, 25th Archbishop of Canterbury, great reformer of common worship, and Anselm, 36th Archbishop, early scholastic theologian, were among notable monastic successors of this far more hierarchical Roman mission. Closer connection to the continent and distance from the Patristic era also meant that from the seventh century onward, British faith and order were increasingly shaped by efforts to create a universal western patriarchate at Rome. The Norman Conquest of the 11th century also played a role in diminishing the distinguishing peculiarities of *Ecclesia Anglicana*. Liturgy also became increasingly complicated and clericalized.

All across Europe, the sixteenth century was marked by reform of the received tradition. So great was this period of reevaluation, especially concerning the primacy of the Holy Scriptures, that the whole era is still known to us as the Reformation.

Archbishop Thomas Cranmer, 69th Archbishop of Canterbury, who was martyred at Oxford in 1556, led the English phase of this reform of Church life and Church worship. Undoubtedly Cranmer's most enduring achievement was his replacement of the numerous books of the Latin liturgy with a carefully compiled *Book of Common Prayer*. This was a Prayer Book in the vernacular, one which brilliantly maintained the traditional patterns of worship, yet which sought to purge away from worship all that was "contrary to Holy Scripture or to the ordering of the Primitive Church." The *Book of Common Prayer*, from the first edition of 1549, became the hallmark of a Christian way of worship and believing that was both catholic and reformed, continuous yet always renewing. According to this pattern, communities of prayer—congregations and families rather than the monasteries of the earliest centuries—would be the centers of formation and of Christ-like service to the world.

For a century, the Church of England matured and broadened as a tradition separated from the Church of Rome. Its pastoral, musical, and ascetical life flourished: Jeremy Taylor, Lancelot Andrewes, Thomas Tallis, William Byrd, and George Herbert are but a few of the names associated with this flowering. Also begun were three centuries of colonial expansion that exported the *Book of Common Prayer* to countless cultures and people-groups the world over.

The English Civil War of the seventeenth century drove the Church of England and her liturgy underground. Nevertheless, with the Restoration of the Monarchy, the *Book of Common Prayer,* authorized by Parliament and Church in 1662, became Anglicanism's *sine qua non.* Great Awakenings and the Methodist movement of the 18th century, as well as adaptations necessary for the first Anglicans independent of the British Crown, challenged and re-shaped Prayer Book worship, as would the East African revival, charismatic renewal, and the dissolution of Empire in the 20th century. Similarly, the evangelical and anglo-catholic movements of the 19th century profoundly affected Anglican self-understanding and worship in different, often seemingly contradictory, ways; yet the *Book of Common Prayer (1662)* was common to every period of this development. For nearly five centuries, Cranmer's Prayer Book idea had endured to shape what emerged as a global Anglican Church that is missional and adaptive as in its earliest centuries; authoritatively Scriptural and creedal as in its greatest season of reform; and evangelical, catholic, and charismatic in its apology and its worship as now globally manifest.

The liturgical movement of the 20th century and the ecumenical *rapprochement* in the second half of that century had an immense impact on the Prayer Book tradition. The *Book of Common Prayer (1979)* in the United States and various Prayer Books that appeared in Anglican Provinces from South America to Kenya to South East Asia to New Zealand were often more revolutionary than evolutionary in character. Eucharistic prayers in particular were influenced by the re-discovery of patristic texts unknown at the Reformation, and often bore little resemblance to what had for centuries been the Anglican norm. Baptismal theology, especially in North America, was affected by radical revisions to the received Christian understanding, and came perilously close to proclaiming a gospel of individual affirmation rather than of personal transformation and sanctification.

At the beginning of the 21st century, global reassessment of the *Book of Common Prayer* of 1662 as "the standard for doctrine, discipline, and worship" shapes the present volume, now presented on the bedrock of its predecessors. Among the timeless treasures offered in this Prayer Book is the Coverdale Psalter of 1535 (employed with every Prayer Book from the mid-16th to the mid-20th centuries), renewed for contemporary use through efforts that included the labors of 20th century Anglicans T. S. Eliot and C. S. Lewis, and brought to final form here. The *Book of Common Prayer (2019)* is indisputably true to Cranmer's originating vision of a form of prayers and praises that is thoroughly Biblical, catholic in the manner of the early centuries, highly participatory in delivery, peculiarly Anglican and English in its roots, culturally adaptive and missional in a most remarkable way, utterly accessible to the people, and whose repetitions are intended to form the faithful catechetically and to give them doxological voice.

The *Book of Common Prayer (2019)* is the product of the new era of reform and restoration that has created the Anglican Church in North America. The Jerusalem Declaration of 2008 located itself within the historic confines of what is authentically the Christian Faith and the Anglican patrimony, and sought to restore their fullness and beauty. The *Book of Common Prayer (2019)* is offered to the same end.

+Foley Beach
Archbishop
Anglican Church in North America
On behalf of the College of Bishops

+Robert Duncan
Archbishop Emeritus
Anglican Church in North America
On behalf of all who shaped this Book

The Feast of the Nativity of St. John the Baptist
ANNO DOMINI MMXIX

DAILY MORNING PRAYER

The Officiant may begin Morning Prayer by reading an opening sentence of Scripture. One of the following, or a sentence from among those provided at the end of the Office (pages 27-29), is customary.

Grace to you and peace from God our Father and the Lord Jesus Christ.   PHILIPPIANS 1:2

or this

I was glad when they said unto me, "We will go into the house of the LORD."   PSALM 122:1

or this

Let the words of my mouth and the meditation of my heart be always acceptable in your sight, O LORD, my rock and my redeemer.   PSALM 19:14

CONFESSION OF SIN

The Officiant says to the People

Dearly beloved, the Scriptures teach us to acknowledge our many sins and offenses, not concealing them from our heavenly Father, but confessing them with humble and obedient hearts that we may obtain forgiveness by his infinite goodness and mercy. We ought at all times humbly to acknowledge our sins before Almighty God, but especially when we come together in his presence to give thanks for the great benefits we have received at his hands, to declare his most worthy praise, to hear his holy Word, and to ask, for ourselves and on behalf of others, those things which are necessary for our life and our salvation. Therefore, draw near with me to the throne of heavenly grace.

or this

Let us humbly confess our sins to Almighty God.

Silence is kept. All kneeling, the Officiant and People say

Almighty and most merciful Father,
    we have erred and strayed from your ways like lost sheep.
We have followed too much the devices and desires
    of our own hearts.
We have offended against your holy laws.
We have left undone those things which we ought to have done,
    and we have done those things which we ought not
    to have done;
    and apart from your grace, there is no health in us.
O Lord, have mercy upon us.
Spare all those who confess their faults.
Restore all those who are penitent, according to your promises
    declared to all people in Christ Jesus our Lord.
And grant, O most merciful Father, for his sake,
    that we may now live a godly, righteous, and sober life,
    to the glory of your holy Name. Amen.

The Priest alone stands and says

Almighty God, the Father of our Lord Jesus Christ, desires not the death of sinners, but that they may turn from their wickedness and live. He has empowered and commanded his ministers to pronounce to his people, being penitent, the absolution and remission of their sins. He pardons and absolves all who truly repent and genuinely believe his holy Gospel. For this reason, we beseech him to grant us true repentance and his Holy Spirit, that our present deeds may please him, the rest of our lives may be pure and holy, and that at the last we may come to his eternal joy; through Jesus Christ our Lord. **Amen.**

or this

The Almighty and merciful Lord grant you absolution and remission of all your sins, true repentance, amendment of life, and the grace and consolation of his Holy Spirit. **Amen.**

A Deacon or layperson remains kneeling and prays

Grant to your faithful people, merciful Lord, pardon and peace; that we may be cleansed from all our sins, and serve you with a quiet mind; through Jesus Christ our Lord. **Amen.**

INVITATORY

All stand.

Officiant	O Lord, open our lips;
People	**And our mouth shall proclaim your praise.**
Officiant	O God, make speed to save us;
People	**O Lord, make haste to help us.**
Officiant	Glory be to the Father, and to the Son, and to the Holy Spirit;
People	**As it was in the beginning, is now, and ever shall be, world without end. Amen.**
Officiant	Praise the Lord.
People	**The Lord's Name be praised.**

Then follows the Venite. Alternatively, the Jubilate may be used.

One of these antiphons, or one from the seasonal antiphons provided at the end of the Office (pages 29-30), may be sung or said before and after the Invitatory Psalm.

The earth is the Lord's for he made it: *
    O come, let us adore him.

or this

Worship the Lord in the beauty of holiness: *
    O come, let us adore him.

or this

The mercy of the Lord is everlasting: *
    O come, let us adore him.

VENITE
O Come

O come, let us sing unto the LORD; *
    let us heartily rejoice in the strength of our salvation.
Let us come before his presence with thanksgiving *
    and show ourselves glad in him with psalms.
For the LORD is a great God *
    and a great King above all gods.
In his hand are all the depths of the earth, *
    and the heights of the hills are his also.
The sea is his, for he made it, *
    and his hands prepared the dry land.
O come, let us worship and fall down, *
    and kneel before the LORD our Maker.
For he is our God, *
    and we are the people of his pasture,
    and the sheep of his hand.

The following verses may be omitted, except in Lent.

Today, if you will hear his voice, harden not your hearts *
    as in the provocation, and as in the day of temptation in
    the wilderness,
When your fathers tested me, *
    and put me to the proof, though they had seen my works.
Forty years long was I grieved with this generation and said, *
    "It is a people that err in their hearts,
    for they have not known my ways,"
Of whom I swore in my wrath *
    that they should not enter into my rest.

PSALM 95:1-7, 8-11

or this

JUBILATE
Be Joyful

O be joyful in the LORD, all you lands; *
    serve the LORD with gladness,
    and come before his presence with a song.
Be assured that the LORD, he is God; *
    it is he that has made us, and not we ourselves;
    we are his people, and the sheep of his pasture.
O go your way into his gates with thanksgiving,
and into his courts with praise; *
    be thankful unto him, and speak good of his Name.
For the LORD is gracious, his mercy is everlasting, *
    and his truth endures from generation to generation.

PSALM 100

*During the first week of Easter, the Pascha Nostrum, without antiphons, is used
in place of the Invitatory Psalm, and it may be used throughout Eastertide.*

13

PASCHA NOSTRUM
Christ our Passover

Alleluia. Christ our Passover has been sacrificed for us; *
 therefore let us keep the feast,
Not with the old leaven, the leaven of malice and evil, *
 but with the unleavened bread of sincerity and truth. Alleluia.
Christ being raised from the dead will never die again; *
 death no longer has dominion over him.
The death that he died, he died to sin, once for all; *
 but the life he lives, he lives to God.
So also consider yourselves dead to sin, *
 and alive to God in Jesus Christ our Lord. Alleluia.
Christ has been raised from the dead, *
 the firstfruits of those who have fallen asleep.
For since by a man came death, *
 by a man has come also the resurrection of the dead.
For as in Adam all die, *
 so also in Christ shall all be made alive. Alleluia.

I CORINTHIANS 5:7-8; ROMANS 6:9-11; I CORINTHIANS 15:20-22

Then follows

THE PSALM OR PSALMS APPOINTED

At the end of the Psalms the Gloria Patri (Glory be...) is sung or said

Glory be to the Father, and to the Son, and to the Holy Spirit; *
 as it was in the beginning, is now, and ever shall be,
 world without end. Amen.

One or more Lessons, as appointed, are read, the Reader first saying

A Reading from _____.

A citation giving chapter and verse may be added.

After each lesson the Reader may say

The Word of the Lord.
People **Thanks be to God.**

Or the Reader may say

Here ends the Reading.

The following Canticles are normally sung or said after each of the lessons. The Officiant may also use a Canticle drawn from the Supplemental Canticles (pages 79-88) or an appropriate song of praise.

TE DEUM LAUDAMUS
We Praise You, O God

We praise you, O God; we acclaim you as Lord; *
    all creation worships you, the Father everlasting.
To you all angels, all the powers of heaven, *
    the cherubim and seraphim, sing in endless praise:
Holy, Holy, Holy, Lord God of power and might, *
    heaven and earth are full of your glory.
The glorious company of apostles praise you. *
    The noble fellowship of prophets praise you.
The white-robed army of martyrs praise you. *
    Throughout the world the holy Church acclaims you:
Father, of majesty unbounded,
your true and only Son, worthy of all praise, *
    and the Holy Spirit, advocate and guide.

You, Christ, are the king of glory, *
 the eternal Son of the Father.
When you took our flesh to set us free *
 you humbly chose the Virgin's womb.
You overcame the sting of death *
 and opened the kingdom of heaven to all believers.
You are seated at God's right hand in glory. *
 We believe that you will come to be our judge.
Come then, Lord, and help your people, *
 bought with the price of your own blood,
and bring us with your saints *
 to glory everlasting.

The following verses may be omitted

Save your people, Lord, and bless your inheritance; *
 govern and uphold them now and always.
Day by day we bless you; *
 we praise your Name for ever.
Keep us today, Lord, from all sin; *
 have mercy on us, Lord, have mercy.
Lord, show us your love and mercy, *
 for we have put our trust in you.
In you, Lord, is our hope; *
 let us never be put to shame.

During Lent the Benedictus es, Domine usually replaces the Te Deum, and it may be used at other times.

BENEDICTUS ES, DOMINE
A Song of Praise

Glory to you, Lord God of our fathers; *
 you are worthy of praise; glory to you.

Glory to you for the radiance of your holy Name; *
  we will praise you and highly exalt you for ever.
Glory to you in the splendor of your temple; *
  on the throne of your majesty, glory to you.
Glory to you, seated between the Cherubim; *
  we will praise you and highly exalt you for ever.
Glory to you, beholding the depths; *
  in the high vault of heaven, glory to you.
Glory to you, Father, Son, and Holy Spirit; *
  we will praise you and highly exalt you for ever.

SONG OF THE THREE YOUNG MEN, 29-34

BENEDICTUS
The Song of Zechariah

Blessed be the Lord, the God of Israel; *
  he has come to his people and set them free.
He has raised up for us a mighty savior, *
  born of the house of his servant David.
Through his holy prophets he promised of old
that he would save us from our enemies, *
  from the hands of all who hate us.
He promised to show mercy to our fathers *
  and to remember his holy covenant.
This was the oath he swore to our father Abraham, *
  to set us free from the hands of our enemies,
Free to worship him without fear, *
  holy and righteous in his sight
  all the days of our life.
You, my child, shall be called the prophet of the Most High, *
  for you will go before the Lord to prepare his way,
To give his people knowledge of salvation *
  by the forgiveness of their sins.

In the tender compassion of our God *
    the dawn from on high shall break upon us,
To shine on those who dwell in darkness
and in the shadow of death, *
    and to guide our feet into the way of peace.

Glory be to the Father, and to the Son, and to the Holy Spirit; *
    as it was in the beginning, is now, and ever shall be,
    world without end. Amen.

LUKE 1:68-79

THE APOSTLES' CREED

Officiant and People together, all standing

I believe in God, the Father almighty,
    creator of heaven and earth.
I believe in Jesus Christ, his only Son, our Lord.
    He was conceived by the Holy Spirit
    and born of the Virgin Mary.
    He suffered under Pontius Pilate,
    was crucified, died, and was buried.
    He descended to the dead.
    On the third day he rose again.
    He ascended into heaven,
    and is seated at the right hand of the Father.
    He will come again to judge the living and the dead.
I believe in the Holy Spirit,
    the holy catholic Church,
    the communion of saints,
    the forgiveness of sins,
    the resurrection of the body,
    and the life everlasting. Amen.

Officiant	The Lord be with you.
People	**And with your spirit.**
Officiant	Let us pray.

The People kneel or stand.

Lord, have mercy upon us.	Lord, have mercy.
Christ, have mercy upon us. *or*	**Christ, have mercy.**
Lord, have mercy upon us.	Lord, have mercy.

Officiant and People

Our Father, who art in heaven,
   hallowed be thy Name,
   thy kingdom come,
   thy will be done,
   on earth as it is in heaven.
Give us this day our daily bread.
And forgive us our trespasses,
   as we forgive those
   who trespass against us.
And lead us not into temptation,
   but deliver us from evil.
For thine is the kingdom,
   and the power, and the glory,
   for ever and ever. Amen.

Our Father in heaven,
   hallowed be your Name,
   your kingdom come,
   your will be done,
   on earth as it is in heaven.
Give us today our daily bread.
And forgive us our sins
   as we forgive those
   who sin against us.
Save us from the time of trial,
   and deliver us from evil.
For the kingdom, the power,
   and the glory are yours,
   now and for ever. Amen.

Officiant	O Lord, show your mercy upon us;
People	**And grant us your salvation.**
Officiant	O Lord, guide those who govern us;
People	**And lead us in the way of justice and truth.**
Officiant	Clothe your ministers with righteousness;
People	**And let your people sing with joy.**

Officiant	O Lord, save your people;
People	**And bless your inheritance.**
Officiant	Give peace in our time, O Lord;
People	**And defend us by your mighty power.**
Officiant	Let not the needy, O Lord, be forgotten;
People	**Nor the hope of the poor be taken away.**
Officiant	Create in us clean hearts, O God;
People	**And take not your Holy Spirit from us.**

The Officiant then prays one or more of the following Collects, always beginning with the Collect of the Day (usually the Collect of the Sunday or Principal Feast and of any of the weekdays following, or of the Holy Day being observed), found on pages 598-640. It is traditional to pray the Collects for Peace and Grace daily. Alternatively, one may pray the Collects on a weekly rotation, using the suggestions in italics.

THE COLLECT OF THE DAY
From the Collects of the Christian Year

A COLLECT FOR STRENGTH TO AWAIT CHRIST'S RETURN
Sunday

O God our King, by the resurrection of your Son Jesus Christ on the first day of the week, you conquered sin, put death to flight, and gave us the hope of everlasting life: Redeem all our days by this victory; forgive our sins, banish our fears, make us bold to praise you and to do your will; and steel us to wait for the consummation of your kingdom on the last great Day; through Jesus Christ our Lord. **Amen.**

A COLLECT FOR THE RENEWAL OF LIFE *Monday*

O God, the King eternal, whose light divides the day from the night and turns the shadow of death into the morning: Drive far from us all wrong desires, incline our hearts to keep your law, and guide our feet into the way of peace; that, having done your will with cheerfulness during the day, we may, when night comes, rejoice to give you thanks; through Jesus Christ our Lord. **Amen**.

A COLLECT FOR PEACE *Tuesday*

O God, the author of peace and lover of concord, to know you is eternal life and to serve you is perfect freedom: Defend us, your humble servants, in all assaults of our enemies; that we, surely trusting in your defense, may not fear the power of any adversaries, through the might of Jesus Christ our Lord. **Amen**.

A COLLECT FOR GRACE *Wednesday*

O Lord, our heavenly Father, almighty and everlasting God, you have brought us safely to the beginning of this day: Defend us by your mighty power, that we may not fall into sin nor run into any danger; and that, guided by your Spirit, we may do what is righteous in your sight; through Jesus Christ our Lord. **Amen**.

A COLLECT FOR GUIDANCE *Thursday*

Heavenly Father, in you we live and move and have our being: We humbly pray you so to guide and govern us by your Holy Spirit, that in all the cares and occupations of our life we may not forget you, but may remember that we are ever walking in your sight; through Jesus Christ our Lord. **Amen**.

A COLLECT FOR ENDURANCE *Friday*

Almighty God, whose most dear Son went not up to joy but first he suffered pain, and entered not into glory before he was crucified: Mercifully grant that we, walking in the way of the Cross, may find it none other than the way of life and peace; through Jesus Christ your Son our Lord. **Amen**.

Almighty God, who after the creation of the world rested from all your works and sanctified a day of rest for all your creatures: Grant that we, putting away all earthly anxieties, may be duly prepared for the service of your sanctuary, and that our rest here upon earth may be a preparation for the eternal rest promised to your people in heaven; through Jesus Christ our Lord. **Amen.**

Unless the Great Litany or the Eucharist is to follow, one of the following prayers for mission is added. If the Great Litany is used, it follows here, or after a hymn or anthem, and concludes the Office.

PRAYER FOR MISSION

Almighty and everlasting God, who alone works great marvels: Send down upon our clergy and the congregations committed to their charge the life-giving Spirit of your grace, shower them with the continual dew of your blessing, and ignite in them a zealous love of your Gospel; through Jesus Christ our Lord. **Amen.**

or this

O God, you have made of one blood all the peoples of the earth, and sent your blessed Son to preach peace to those who are far off and to those who are near: Grant that people everywhere may seek after you and find you; bring the nations into your fold; pour out your Spirit upon all flesh; and hasten the coming of your kingdom; through Jesus Christ our Lord. **Amen.**

or this

Lord Jesus Christ, you stretched out your arms of love on the hard wood of the Cross that everyone might come within the reach of your saving embrace: So clothe us in your Spirit that we, reaching forth our hands in love, may bring those who do not know you to the knowledge and love of you; for the honor of your Name. **Amen.**

The Officiant may invite the People to offer intercessions and thanksgivings.

A hymn or anthem may be sung.

Before the close of the Office one or both of the following prayers may be used.

THE GENERAL THANKSGIVING

Officiant and People

Almighty God, Father of all mercies,
    we your unworthy servants give you humble thanks
    for all your goodness and loving-kindness
    to us and to all whom you have made.
We bless you for our creation, preservation,
    and all the blessings of this life;
    but above all for your immeasurable love
    in the redemption of the world by our Lord Jesus Christ;
    for the means of grace, and for the hope of glory.
And, we pray, give us such an awareness of your mercies,
    that with truly thankful hearts
    we may show forth your praise,
    not only with our lips, but in our lives,
    by giving up our selves to your service,
    and by walking before you
    in holiness and righteousness all our days;
Through Jesus Christ our Lord,
    to whom, with you and the Holy Spirit,
    be honor and glory throughout all ages. Amen.

Almighty God, you have given us grace at this time, with one accord to make our common supplications to you; and you have promised through your well-beloved Son that when two or three are gathered together in his Name you will grant their requests: Fulfill now, O Lord, our desires and petitions as may be best for us; granting us in this world knowledge of your truth, and in the age to come life everlasting. **Amen.**

Officiant   Let us bless the Lord.
People   **Thanks be to God.**

From Easter Day through the Day of Pentecost, "Alleluia, alleluia" may be added to the preceding versicle and response.

The Officiant says one of these concluding sentences (and the People may be invited to join)

The grace of our Lord Jesus Christ, and the love of God, and the fellowship of the Holy Spirit, be with us all evermore. **Amen.**   2 CORINTHIANS 13:14[T]

May the God of hope fill us with all joy and peace in believing through the power of the Holy Spirit. **Amen.**   ROMANS 15:13[T]

Glory to God whose power, working in us, can do infinitely more than we can ask or imagine: Glory to him from generation to generation in the Church, and in Christ Jesus for ever and ever. **Amen.**   EPHESIANS 3:20-21[T]

OPENING SENTENCES OF SCRIPTURE

ADVENT

In the wilderness prepare the way of the LORD; make straight in the desert a highway for our God.   ISAIAH 40:3

CHRISTMAS

Fear not, for behold, I bring you good news of great joy that will be for all the people. For unto you is born this day in the city of David a Savior, who is Christ the Lord.   LUKE 2:10-11

EPIPHANY

From the rising of the sun to its setting my name will be great among the nations, and in every place incense will be offered to my name, and a pure offering. For my name will be great among the nations, says the LORD of hosts.   MALACHI 1:11

LENT *and* OTHER PENITENTIAL OCCASIONS

Repent, for the kingdom of heaven is at hand.   MATTHEW 3:2

Turn your face from my sins,
    and blot out all my misdeeds.   PSALM 51:9

If anyone would come after me, let him deny himself and take up his cross and follow me.   MARK 8:34

HOLY WEEK

Is it nothing to you, all you who pass by? Look and see
if there is any sorrow like my sorrow, which was brought
upon me, which the LORD inflicted on the day of his
fierce anger.   LAMENTATIONS 1:12

EASTER

If then you have been raised with Christ, seek the things
that are above, where Christ is, seated at the right hand
of God.   COLOSSIANS 3:1

ASCENSION

Since then we have a great high priest who has passed through
the heavens, Jesus, the Son of God, let us hold fast our
confession. Let us then with confidence draw near to the throne
of grace, that we may receive mercy and find grace to help in
time of need.   HEBREWS 4:14, 16

PENTECOST

You will receive power when the Holy Spirit has come upon
you, and you will be my witnesses in Jerusalem and in all Judea
and Samaria, and to the end of the earth.   ACTS 1:8

TRINITY SUNDAY

Holy, holy, holy, is the Lord God Almighty, who was and is and
is to come!   REVELATION 4:8

DAYS OF THANKSGIVING

Honor the LORD with your wealth and with the firstfruits of all
your produce; then your barns will be filled with plenty, and your
vats will be bursting with wine.   PROVERBS 3:9-10

AT ANY TIME

The LORD is in his holy temple; let all the earth keep silence
before him.   HABAKKUK 2:20

O send out your light and your truth, that they may lead me, and bring me to your holy hill, and to your dwelling.   PSALM 43:3

Thus says the One who is high and lifted up, who inhabits eternity, whose name is Holy: "I dwell in the high and holy place, and also with him who is of a contrite and lowly spirit, to revive the spirit of the lowly, and to revive the heart of the contrite."   ISAIAH 57:15

The hour is coming, and is now here, when the true worshipers will worship the Father in spirit and truth, for the Father is seeking such people to worship him.   JOHN 4:23

SEASONAL ANTIPHONS

ADVENT

Our King and Savior now draws near: *
   O come, let us adore him.

CHRISTMAS

Alleluia. Unto us a child is born: *
   O come, let us adore him. Alleluia.

EPIPHANY, *and* THE FEAST OF THE TRANSFIGURATION

The Lord has shown forth his glory: *
   O come, let us adore him.

PRESENTATION *and* ANNUNCIATION

The Word was made flesh and dwelt among us: *
   O come, let us adore him.

The Lord is full of compassion and mercy: *
   O come, let us adore him.

Alleluia. The Lord is risen indeed: *
   O come, let us adore him. Alleluia.

Alleluia. Christ the Lord has ascended into heaven: *
   O come, let us adore him. Alleluia.

Alleluia. The Spirit of the Lord renews the face of the earth: *
   O come, let us adore him. Alleluia.

Father, Son, and Holy Spirit, one God: *
   O come, let us adore him.

The Lord is glorious in his saints: *
   O come, let us adore him.

ADDITIONAL DIRECTIONS

The Confession and Apostles' Creed may be omitted, provided each is said at least once during the course of the day.

The Gloria Patri (Glory be...) in the opening versicles may be said in unison. The following form of the Gloria Patri may alternatively be used:
Glory to the Father, and to the Son, and to the Holy Spirit:
 As it was in the beginning, is now, and will be for ever. Amen.

The Officiant and People may join in saying "Alleluia" (except in Lent) as an alternative to the versicles "Praise the Lord. The Lord's Name be praised."

If an offering is to be received, it is appropriate to do so during the hymn or anthem following the Collects.

A sermon may be preached after the lessons, after the hymn or anthem following the Collects, or after the conclusion of the Office.

DAILY EVENING PRAYER

The Officiant may begin Evening Prayer by reading an opening sentence of Scripture. One of the following, or a sentence from among those provided at the end of the Office (pages 54-56), is customary.

Jesus spoke to them, saying, "I am the light of the world. Whoever follows me will not walk in darkness, but will have the light of life." JOHN 8:12

or this

LORD, I have loved the habitation of your house and the place where your honor dwells. PSALM 26:8

or this

Let my prayer be set forth in your sight as incense, and let the lifting up of my hands be an evening sacrifice. PSALM 141:2

CONFESSION OF SIN

The Officiant says to the People

Dearly beloved, the Scriptures teach us to acknowledge our many sins and offenses, not concealing them from our heavenly Father, but confessing them with humble and obedient hearts that we may obtain forgiveness by his infinite goodness and mercy. We ought at all times humbly to acknowledge our sins before Almighty God, but especially when we come together in his presence to give thanks for the great benefits we have received at his hands, to declare his most worthy praise, to hear his holy Word, and to ask, for ourselves and on behalf of others, those things which are necessary for our life and our salvation. Therefore, draw near with me to the throne of heavenly grace.

or this

Let us humbly confess our sins to Almighty God.

Silence is kept. All kneeling, the Officiant and People say

Almighty and most merciful Father,
   we have erred and strayed from your ways like lost sheep.
We have followed too much the devices and desires
   of our own hearts.
We have offended against your holy laws.
We have left undone those things which we ought to have done,
   and we have done those things which we ought not
   to have done;
   and apart from your grace, there is no health in us.
O Lord, have mercy upon us.
Spare all those who confess their faults.
Restore all those who are penitent, according to your promises
   declared to all people in Christ Jesus our Lord.
And grant, O most merciful Father, for his sake,
   that we may now live a godly, righteous, and sober life,
   to the glory of your holy Name. Amen.

The Priest alone stands and says

Almighty God, the Father of our Lord Jesus Christ, desires not the death of sinners, but that they may turn from their wickedness and live. He has empowered and commanded his ministers to pronounce to his people, being penitent, the absolution and remission of their sins. He pardons and absolves all who truly repent and genuinely believe his holy Gospel. For this reason, we beseech him to grant us true repentance and his Holy Spirit, that our present deeds may please him, the rest of our lives may be pure and holy, and that at the last we may come to his eternal joy; through Jesus Christ our Lord. **Amen.**

or this

The Almighty and merciful Lord grant you absolution and remission of all your sins, true repentance, amendment of life, and the grace and consolation of his Holy Spirit. **Amen.**

A Deacon or layperson remains kneeling and prays

Grant to your faithful people, merciful Lord, pardon and peace; that we may be cleansed from all our sins, and serve you with a quiet mind; through Jesus Christ our Lord. **Amen.**

THE INVITATORY

All stand.

Officiant	O Lord, open our lips;
People	**And our mouth shall proclaim your praise.**
Officiant	O God, make speed to save us;
People	**O Lord, make haste to help us.**
Officiant	Glory be to the Father, and to the Son, and to the Holy Spirit;
People	**As it was in the beginning, is now, and ever shall be, world without end. Amen.**
Officiant	Praise the Lord.
People	**The Lord's Name be praised.**

The following or some other suitable hymn or Psalm may be sung or said.

PHOS HILARON
O Gladsome Light

O gladsome light,
pure brightness of the everliving Father in heaven, *
   O Jesus Christ, holy and blessed!
Now as we come to the setting of the sun,
and our eyes behold the vesper light, *
   we sing your praises, O God: Father, Son, and Holy Spirit.
You are worthy at all times to be praised by happy voices, *
   O Son of God, O Giver of Life,
    and to be glorified through all the worlds.

Then follows

THE PSALM OR PSALMS APPOINTED

At the end of the Psalms the Gloria Patri (Glory be…) is sung or said

Glory be to the Father, and to the Son, and to the Holy Spirit; *
   as it was in the beginning, is now, and ever shall be,
   world without end. Amen.

THE LESSONS

One or more Lessons, as appointed, are read, the Reader first saying

   A Reading from _____.

A citation giving chapter and verse may be added.

After each Lesson the Reader may say

   The Word of the Lord.
People   Thanks be to God.

Or the Reader may say

Here ends the Reading.

The following Canticles are normally sung or said after each of the lessons. The Officiant may also use a Canticle drawn from the Supplemental Canticles (pages 79-88) or an appropriate song of praise.

MAGNIFICAT
The Song of Mary

My soul magnifies the Lord, *
    and my spirit rejoices in God my Savior;
For he has regarded *
    the lowliness of his handmaiden.
For behold, from now on, *
    all generations will call me blessed;
For he that is mighty has magnified me, *
    and holy is his Name.
And his mercy is on those who fear him, *
    throughout all generations.
He has shown the strength of his arm; *
    he has scattered the proud in the imagination of their hearts.
He has brought down the mighty from their thrones, *
    and has exalted the humble and meek.
He has filled the hungry with good things, *
    and the rich he has sent empty away.
He, remembering his mercy, has helped his servant Israel, *
    as he promised to our fathers, Abraham and his seed for ever.

Glory be to the Father, and to the Son, and to the Holy Spirit; *
    as it was in the beginning, is now, and ever shall be,
    world without end. Amen.   LUKE 1:46-55

Lord, now let your servant depart in peace, *
    according to your word.
For my eyes have seen your salvation, *
    which you have prepared before the face of all people;
To be a light to lighten the Gentiles, *
    and to be the glory of your people Israel.

Glory be to the Father, and to the Son, and to the Holy Spirit; *
    as it was in the beginning, is now, and ever shall be,
    world without end. Amen.   LUKE 2:29-32

THE APOSTLES' CREED

Officiant and People together, all standing

I believe in God, the Father almighty,
    creator of heaven and earth.
I believe in Jesus Christ, his only Son, our Lord.
    He was conceived by the Holy Spirit
    and born of the Virgin Mary.
    He suffered under Pontius Pilate,
    was crucified, died, and was buried.
    He descended to the dead.
    On the third day he rose again.
    He ascended into heaven,
    and is seated at the right hand of the Father.
    He will come again to judge the living and the dead.
I believe in the Holy Spirit,
    the holy catholic Church,
    the communion of saints,
    the forgiveness of sins,
    the resurrection of the body,
    and the life everlasting. Amen.

Officiant	The Lord be with you.
People	**And with your spirit.**
Officiant	Let us pray.

The People kneel or stand.

Lord, have mercy upon us.		Lord, have mercy.
Christ, have mercy upon us.	*or*	**Christ, have mercy.**
Lord, have mercy upon us.		Lord, have mercy.

Officiant and People

Our Father, who art in heaven,
    hallowed be thy Name,
    thy kingdom come,
    thy will be done,
    on earth as it is in heaven.
Give us this day our daily bread.
And forgive us our trespasses,
    as we forgive those
    who trespass against us.
And lead us not into temptation,
    but deliver us from evil.
For thine is the kingdom,
    and the power, and the glory,
    for ever and ever. Amen.

Our Father in heaven,
    hallowed be your Name,
    your kingdom come,
    your will be done,
    on earth as it is in heaven.
Give us today our daily bread.
And forgive us our sins
    as we forgive those
    who sin against us.
Save us from the time of trial,
    and deliver us from evil.
For the kingdom, the power,
    and the glory are yours,
    now and for ever. Amen.

Then follows one of these sets of Suffrages

Officiant	O Lord, show your mercy upon us;
People	**And grant us your salvation.**
Officiant	O Lord, guide those who govern us;
People	**And lead us in the way of justice and truth.**

Officiant	Clothe your ministers with righteousness;
People	**And let your people sing with joy.**
Officiant	O Lord, save your people;
People	**And bless your inheritance.**
Officiant	Give peace in our time, O Lord;
People	**And defend us by your mighty power.**
Officiant	Let not the needy, O Lord, be forgotten;
People	**Nor the hope of the poor be taken away.**
Officiant	Create in us clean hearts, O God;
People	**And take not your Holy Spirit from us.**

or this

That this evening may be holy, good, and peaceful,
  We entreat you, O Lord.

That your holy angels may lead us in paths of peace and goodwill,
  We entreat you, O Lord.

That we may be pardoned and forgiven for our sins and offenses,
  We entreat you, O Lord.

That there may be peace in your Church and in the whole world,
  We entreat you, O Lord.

That we may depart this life in your faith and fear, and not be
  condemned before the great judgment seat of Christ,
  We entreat you, O Lord.

That we may be bound together by your Holy Spirit in the
  communion of [_____ and] all your saints, entrusting
  one another and all our life to Christ,
  We entreat you, O Lord.

The Officiant then prays one or more of the following Collects, always beginning with the Collect of the Day (usually the Collect of the Sunday or Principal Feast and of any of the weekdays following, or of the Holy Day being observed) found on pages 598-640. It is traditional to pray the Collects for Peace and Aid against Perils daily. Alternatively, one may pray the Collects on a weekly rotation, using the suggestions in italics.

THE COLLECT OF THE DAY
From the Collects of the Christian Year

A COLLECT FOR RESURRECTION HOPE *Sunday*

Lord God, whose Son our Savior Jesus Christ triumphed over the powers of death and prepared for us our place in the new Jerusalem: Grant that we, who have this day given thanks for his resurrection, may praise you in that City of which he is the light, and where he lives and reigns for ever and ever. **Amen.**

A COLLECT FOR PEACE *Monday*

O God, the source of all holy desires, all good counsels, and all just works: Give to your servants that peace which the world cannot give, that our hearts may be set to obey your commandments, and that we, being defended from the fear of our enemies, may pass our time in rest and quietness; through the merits of Jesus Christ our Savior. **Amen.**

A COLLECT FOR AID AGAINST PERILS *Tuesday*

Lighten our darkness, we beseech you, O Lord; and by your great mercy defend us from all perils and dangers of this night; for the love of your only Son, our Savior Jesus Christ. **Amen.**

O God, the life of all who live, the light of the faithful, the strength of those who labor, and the repose of the dead: We thank you for the blessings of the day that is past, and humbly ask for your protection through the coming night. Bring us in safety to the morning hours; through him who died and rose again for us, your Son our Savior Jesus Christ. **Amen.**

A COLLECT FOR THE PRESENCE OF CHRIST *Thursday*

Lord Jesus, stay with us, for evening is at hand and the day is past; be our companion in the way, kindle our hearts, and awaken hope, that we may know you as you are revealed in Scripture and the breaking of bread. Grant this for the sake of your love. **Amen.**

A COLLECT FOR FAITH *Friday*

Lord Jesus Christ, by your death you took away the sting of death: Grant to us your servants so to follow in faith where you have led the way, that we may at length fall asleep peacefully in you and wake up in your likeness; for your tender mercies' sake. **Amen.**

A COLLECT FOR THE EVE OF WORSHIP *Saturday*

O God, the source of eternal light: Shed forth your unending day upon us who watch for you, that our lips may praise you, our lives may bless you, and our worship on the morrow give you glory; through Jesus Christ our Lord. **Amen.**

Unless the Great Litany or the Eucharist is to follow, one of the following prayers for mission is added. If the Great Litany is used, it follows here, or after a hymn or anthem, and concludes the Office.

O God and Father of all, whom the whole heavens adore:
Let the whole earth also worship you, all nations obey you, all
tongues confess and bless you, and men, women, and children
everywhere love you and serve you in peace; through Jesus
Christ our Lord. **Amen.**

or this

Keep watch, dear Lord, with those who work, or watch, or weep
this night, and give your angels charge over those who sleep.
Tend the sick, Lord Christ; give rest to the weary, bless the
dying, soothe the suffering, pity the afflicted, shield the joyous;
and all for your love's sake. **Amen.**

or this

O God, you manifest in your servants the signs of your
presence: Send forth upon us the Spirit of love, that in
companionship with one another your abounding grace may
increase among us; through Jesus Christ our Lord. **Amen.**

The Officiant may invite the People to offer intercessions and thanksgivings.

A hymn or anthem may be sung.

Before the close of the Office one or both of the following prayers may be used.

THE GENERAL THANKSGIVING

Officiant and People

Almighty God, Father of all mercies,
 we your unworthy servants give you humble thanks
 for all your goodness and loving-kindness
 to us and to all whom you have made.

We bless you for our creation, preservation,
  and all the blessings of this life;
    but above all for your immeasurable love
    in the redemption of the world by our Lord Jesus Christ;
    for the means of grace, and for the hope of glory.
And, we pray, give us such an awareness of your mercies,
    that with truly thankful hearts we may show forth your praise,
    not only with our lips, but in our lives,
    by giving up our selves to your service,
    and by walking before you
    in holiness and righteousness all our days;
Through Jesus Christ our Lord,
    to whom, with you and the Holy Spirit,
    be honor and glory throughout all ages. Amen.

A PRAYER OF ST. JOHN CHRYSOSTOM

Almighty God, you have given us grace at this time, with one
accord to make our common supplications to you; and you have
promised through your well-beloved Son that when two or three
are gathered together in his Name you will grant their requests:
Fulfill now, O Lord, our desires and petitions as may be best for
us; granting us in this world knowledge of your truth, and in the
age to come life everlasting. **Amen.**

Officiant   Let us bless the Lord.
  People   **Thanks be to God.**

*From Easter Day through the Day of Pentecost, "Alleluia, alleluia" may be added
to the preceding versicle and response.*

*The Officiant says one of these concluding sentences (and the People may be
invited to join)*

The grace of our Lord Jesus Christ, and the love of God, and the fellowship of the Holy Spirit, be with us all evermore. **Amen.**

2 CORINTHIANS 13:14[T]

May the God of hope fill us with all joy and peace in believing through the power of the Holy Spirit. **Amen.**

ROMANS 15:13[T]

Glory to God whose power, working in us, can do infinitely more than we can ask or imagine: Glory to him from generation to generation in the Church, and in Christ Jesus for ever and ever. **Amen.**

EPHESIANS 3:20-21[T]

OPENING SENTENCES OF SCRIPTURE

ADVENT

Therefore stay awake—for you do not know when the master of the house will come, in the evening, or at midnight, or when the rooster crows, or in the morning—lest he come suddenly and find you asleep. MARK 13:35-36

CHRISTMAS

Behold, the dwelling place of God is with man. He will dwell with them, and they will be his people, and God himself will be with them as their God. REVELATION 21:3

EPIPHANY

Nations shall come to your light, and kings to the brightness of your rising. ISAIAH 60:3

LENT *and* OTHER PENITENTIAL OCCASIONS

If we say we have no sin, we deceive ourselves, and the truth is not in us. If we confess our sins, he is faithful and just to forgive us our sins and to cleanse us from all unrighteousness. I JOHN 1:8-9

For I acknowledge my faults,
 and my sin is ever before me. PSALM 51:3

To the Lord our God belong mercy and forgiveness, for we have rebelled against him. DANIEL 9:9

HOLY WEEK

All we like sheep have gone astray; we have turned every one to his own way; and the LORD has laid on him the iniquity of us all.
ISAIAH 53:6

EASTER

Thanks be to God, who gives us the victory through our Lord Jesus Christ.
1 CORINTHIANS 15:57

ASCENSION

For Christ has entered, not into holy places made with hands, which are copies of the true things, but into heaven itself, now to appear in the presence of God on our behalf.
HEBREWS 9:24

PENTECOST

The Spirit and the Bride say, "Come." And let the one who hears say, "Come." And let the one who is thirsty come; let the one who desires take the water of life without price.
REVELATION 22:17

There is a river whose streams make glad the city of God, the holy dwelling place of the Most High.
PSALM 46:4

TRINITY SUNDAY

Holy, holy, holy is the LORD of Hosts; the whole earth is full of his glory!
ISAIAH 6:3

DAYS OF THANKSGIVING

The LORD by wisdom founded the earth; by understanding he established the heavens; by his knowledge the deeps broke open, and the clouds drop down the dew.
PROVERBS 3:19-20

O worship the Lord in the beauty of holiness;
    let the whole earth stand in awe of him.   PSALM 96:9

I will thank the Lord for giving me counsel;
    my heart also chastens me in the night season.
I have set the Lord always before me;
    he is at my right hand; therefore I shall not fall.   PSALM 16:8-9

ADDITIONAL DIRECTIONS

The Confession and Apostles' Creed may be omitted, provided each is said at least once during the course of the day.

The Gloria Patri (Glory be...) in the opening versicles may be said in unison. The following form of the Gloria Patri may alternatively be used:

Glory to the Father, and to the Son, and to the Holy Spirit:
    As it was in the beginning, is now, and will be for ever. Amen.

The Officiant and People may join in saying "Alleluia" (except in Lent) as an alternative to the versicles "Praise the Lord. The Lord's Name be praised."

If an offering is to be received, it is appropriate to do so during the hymn or anthem following the Collects.

A sermon may be preached after the lessons, after the hymn or anthem following the Collects, or after the conclusion of the Office.

COMPLINE

The Officiant begins

The Lord Almighty grant us a peaceful night
   and a perfect end. **Amen.**

Officiant Our help is in the Name of the Lord;
People **The maker of heaven and earth.**

The Officiant continues

Let us humbly confess our sins to Almighty God.

Silence may be kept. The Officiant and People then say

Almighty God and Father, we confess to you,
to one another, and to the whole company of heaven,
   that we have sinned, through our own fault,
   in thought, and word, and deed,
   and in what we have left undone.
For the sake of your Son our Lord Jesus Christ,
   have mercy upon us, forgive us our sins,
   and by the power of your Holy Spirit
   raise us up to serve you in newness of life,
   to the glory of your Name. Amen.

The Officiant alone says

May Almighty God grant us forgiveness of all our sins,
and the grace and comfort of the Holy Spirit. **Amen.**

Officiant	O God, make speed to save us;
People	**O Lord, make haste to help us.**
Officiant	Glory be to the Father, and to the Son, and to the Holy Spirit;
People	**As it was in the beginning, is now, and ever shall be, world without end. Amen.**

Except in Lent, add **Alleluia.**

One or more of the following, or some other suitable Psalm, is sung or said.

PSALM 4
Cum invocarem

1 Hear me when I call, O God of my righteousness; *
    you set me free when I was in trouble; have mercy upon me,
    and hear my prayer.
2 O you children of men, how long will you blaspheme
    my honor, *
    and have such pleasure in vanity, and seek after falsehood?
3 Know this also, that the Lord has chosen for himself
    the one that is godly; *
    when I call upon the Lord, he will hear me.
4 Stand in awe, and sin not; *
    commune with your own heart upon your bed, and be still.
5 Offer the sacrifice of righteousness *
    and put your trust in the Lord.
6 There are many that say, "Who will show us any good?" *
    Lord, lift up the light of your countenance upon us.

7 You have put gladness in my heart, *
    more than when others' grain and wine and oil increased.
8 I will lay me down in peace, and take my rest; *
    for you, LORD, only, make me dwell in safety.

PSALM 31:1-6
In te, Domine, speravi

1 In you, O LORD, have I put my trust; *
    let me never be put to confusion;
    deliver me in your righteousness.
2 Bow down your ear to me, *
    make haste to deliver me,
3 And be my strong rock and house of defense, *
    that you may save me.
4 For you are my strong rock and my castle; *
    be also my guide, and lead me for your Name's sake.
5 Draw me out of the net that they have laid secretly for me, *
    for you are my strength.
6 Into your hands I commend my spirit, *
    for you have redeemed me, O LORD, O God of truth.

PSALM 91
Qui habitat

1 Whoever dwells under the defense of the Most High *
    shall abide under the shadow of the Almighty.
2 I will say unto the LORD, "You are my refuge and
my stronghold, *
    my God in whom I will trust."
3 For he shall deliver you from the snare of the hunter *
    and from the deadly pestilence.
4 He shall defend you under his wings, and you shall be safe
under his feathers; *
    his faithfulness and truth shall be your shield and buckler.

5 You shall not be afraid of any terror by night, *
       nor of the arrow that flies by day,
6 Of the pestilence that walks in darkness, *
       nor of the sickness that destroys at noonday.
7 A thousand shall fall beside you, and ten thousand
   at your right hand, *
       but it shall not come near you.
8 Indeed, with your eyes you shall behold *
       and see the reward of the ungodly.
9 Because you have said, "The LORD is my refuge," *
       and have made the Most High your stronghold,
10 There shall no evil happen to you, *
       neither shall any plague come near your dwelling.
11 For he shall give his angels charge over you, *
       to keep you in all your ways.
12 They shall bear you in their hands, *
       that you hurt not your foot against a stone.
13 You shall tread upon the lion and adder; *
       the young lion and the serpent you shall trample
       under your feet.
14 "Because he has set his love upon me, therefore I will
   deliver him; *
       I will lift him up, because he has known my Name.
15 He shall call upon me, and I will hear him; *
       indeed, I am with him in trouble; I will deliver him
       and bring him honor.
16 With long life I will satisfy him, *
       and show him my salvation."

PSALM 134
Ecce nunc

1 Behold now, praise the LORD, *
       all you servants of the LORD,

² You that stand by night in the house of the LORD, *
    even in the courts of the house of our God.
³ Lift up your hands in the sanctuary *
    and sing praises unto the LORD.
⁴ The LORD who made heaven and earth *
    give you blessing out of Zion.

At the end of the Psalms the Gloria Patri (Glory be...) is sung or said

Glory be to the Father, and to the Son, and to the Holy Spirit;
    as it was in the beginning, is now, and ever shall be,
    world without end. Amen.

One of the following, or some other suitable passage of Scripture, is read

You, O LORD, are in the midst of us, and we are called by your name; do not leave us. JEREMIAH 14:9

Come to me, all who labor and are heavy laden, and I will give you rest. Take my yoke upon you, and learn from me, for I am gentle and lowly in heart, and you will find rest for your souls. For my yoke is easy, and my burden is light. MATTHEW 11:28-30

Now may the God of peace who brought again from the dead our Lord Jesus, the great shepherd of the sheep, by the blood of the eternal covenant, equip you with everything good that you may do his will, working in us that which is pleasing in his sight, through Jesus Christ, to whom be glory forever and ever. Amen. HEBREWS 13:20-21

Be sober-minded; be watchful. Your adversary the devil prowls around like a roaring lion, seeking someone to devour. Resist him, firm in your faith. 1 PETER 5:8-9

        The Word of the Lord.
People **Thanks be to God.**

A period of silence may follow. A suitable hymn may be sung.

Officiant Into your hands, O Lord, I commend my spirit;
People **For you have redeemed me, O Lord, O God of truth.**
Officiant Keep me, O Lord, as the apple of your eye;
People **Hide me under the shadow of your wings.**

Lord, have mercy upon us.		Lord, have mercy.
Christ, have mercy upon us.	*or*	**Christ, have mercy.**
Lord, have mercy upon us.		Lord, have mercy.

Officiant and People

Our Father, who art in heaven,
    hallowed be thy Name,
    thy kingdom come,
    thy will be done,
    on earth as it is in heaven.
Give us this day our daily bread.
And forgive us our trespasses,
    as we forgive those
    who trespass against us.
And lead us not into temptation,
    but deliver us from evil.
For thine is the kingdom,
    and the power, and the glory,
    for ever and ever. Amen.

Our Father in heaven,
    hallowed be your Name,
    your kingdom come,
    your will be done,
    on earth as it is in heaven.
Give us today our daily bread.
And forgive us our sins
    as we forgive those
    who sin against us.
Save us from the time of trial,
    and deliver us from evil.
For the kingdom, the power,
    and the glory are yours,
    now and for ever. Amen.

Officiant	O Lord, hear our prayer;
People	**And let our cry come to you.**
Officiant	Let us pray.

The Officiant then says one or more of the following Collects. Other appropriate Collects may also be used.

Visit this place, O Lord, and drive far from it all snares of the enemy; let your holy angels dwell with us to preserve us in peace; and let your blessing be upon us always; through Jesus Christ our Lord. **Amen.**

Lighten our darkness, we beseech you, O Lord; and by your great mercy defend us from all perils and dangers of this night; for the love of your only Son, our Savior Jesus Christ. **Amen.**

Be present, O merciful God, and protect us through the hours of this night, so that we who are wearied by the changes and chances of this life may rest in your eternal changelessness; through Jesus Christ our Lord. **Amen.**

Look down, O Lord, from your heavenly throne, illumine this night with your celestial brightness, and from the children of light banish the deeds of darkness; through Jesus Christ our Lord. **Amen.**

A COLLECT FOR SATURDAYS

We give you thanks, O God, for revealing your Son Jesus Christ to us by the light of his resurrection: Grant that as we sing your glory at the close of this day, our joy may abound in the morning as we celebrate the Paschal mystery; through Jesus Christ our Lord. **Amen.**

One of the following prayers may be added

Keep watch, dear Lord, with those who work, or watch, or weep this night, and give your angels charge over those who sleep. Tend the sick, Lord Christ; give rest to the weary, bless the dying, soothe the suffering, pity the afflicted, shield the joyous; and all for your love's sake. **Amen.**

or this

O God, your unfailing providence sustains the world we live in and the life we live: Watch over those, both night and day, who work while others sleep, and grant that we may never forget that our common life depends upon each other's toil; through Jesus Christ our Lord. **Amen.**

Silence may be kept, and other intercessions and thanksgivings may be offered.

The Officiant and People say or sing the Song of Simeon with this Antiphon

Guide us waking, O Lord, and guard us sleeping; that awake we may watch with Christ, and asleep we may rest in peace.

In Easter Season, add   **Alleluia, alleluia, alleluia.**

NUNC DIMITTIS
The Song of Simeon

Lord, now let your servant depart in peace, *
   according to your word.
For my eyes have seen your salvation, *
   which you have prepared before the face of all people;
To be a light to lighten the Gentiles, *
   and to be the glory of your people Israel.

Glory be to the Father, and to the Son, and to the Holy Spirit; *
   as it was in the beginning, is now, and ever shall be,
   world without end. Amen.   LUKE 2:29-32

Guide us waking, O Lord, and guard us sleeping; that awake we may watch with Christ, and asleep we may rest in peace.

In Easter Season, add Alleluia, alleluia, alleluia.

Officiant Let us bless the Lord.
People Thanks be to God.

The Officiant concludes with the following

The almighty and merciful Lord, Father, Son, and Holy Spirit, bless us and keep us, this night and evermore. **Amen.**

ADDITIONAL DIRECTIONS

A Bishop or Priest, if present, may pronounce absolution after the confession.

For those saying Compline every day, particularly in families or other communities, additional short Scriptural readings may be desired. Some appropriate readings include:

ISAIAH 26:3-4
ISAIAH 30:15
MATTHEW 6:31-34
2 CORINTHIANS 4:6
1 THESSALONIANS 5:9-10
1 THESSALONIANS 5:23
EPHESIANS 4:26-27

Either version of the Lord's Prayer may be ended with, "deliver us from evil. Amen." omitting the concluding doxology.

CONCERNING FAMILY PRAYER

These devotions follow the basic structure of the Daily Office of the Church and are particularly appropriate for families with young children.

The Reading and the Collect may be read by one person, and the other parts said in unison, or in some other convenient manner.

Appropriate Opening Sentences, Psalms, Readings, and Collects are provided in each service. When desired, however, the Collect of the Day, or any of the Collects appointed in the Daily Office, may be used instead. The Opening Sentences may be replaced by those appointed for various seasons in the liturgies for Morning and Evening Prayer.

The Psalms and Readings may be replaced by those appointed in:
    the Sunday, Holy Days and Commemoration Lectionary; or
    the Daily Office Lectionary; or
    some other manual of devotion which provides daily selections
    for the Church Year.

A concluding sentence from Morning or Evening Prayer may be used at the end of any of these devotions.

FAMILY PRAYER
IN THE MORNING

The following or some other verse of Scripture is said

O Lord, open my lips,
    and my mouth shall show forth your praise.   PSALM 51:15

PSALM 51:10-12

¹⁰ Create in me a clean heart, O God, *
    and renew a right spirit within me.
¹¹ Cast me not away from your presence, *
    and take not your holy Spirit from me.
¹² O give me the comfort of your help again, *
    and sustain me with your willing Spirit.

Glory be to the Father, and to the Son, and to the Holy Spirit: *
    as it was in the beginning, is now, and ever shall be,
    world without end. Amen.

Alternatively, Psalm 5:1-3 may be used.

A READING FROM HOLY SCRIPTURE

Blessed be the God and Father of our Lord Jesus Christ!
According to his great mercy, he has caused us to be born again

to a living hope through the resurrection of Jesus Christ from
the dead.   I PETER 1:3

or this

Give thanks to the Father, who has qualified you to share in
the inheritance of the saints in light. He has delivered us from
the domain of darkness and transferred us to the kingdom of
his beloved Son, in whom we have redemption, the forgiveness
of sins.   COLOSSIANS 1:12-14

or this

If then you have been raised with Christ, seek the things that
are above, where Christ is, seated at the right hand of God. Set
your minds on things that are above, not on things that are on
earth. For you have died, and your life is hidden with Christ in
God. When Christ who is your life appears, then you also will
appear with him in glory.   COLOSSIANS 3:1-4

A period of silence may follow.

A hymn or canticle may be used; the Apostles' Creed (page 75) may be said.

Prayers may be offered for ourselves and others.

THE LORD'S PRAYER

THE COLLECT

O Lord, our heavenly Father, almighty and everlasting God, you
have brought us safely to the beginning of this day: Defend us
by your mighty power, that we may not fall into sin nor run into
any danger; and that, guided by your Spirit, we may do what is
righteous in your sight; through Jesus Christ our Lord. **Amen.**

The following or some other verse of Scripture is said

Blessed be the God and Father of our Lord Jesus Christ, who has blessed us in Christ with every spiritual blessing in the heavenly places.   EPHESIANS 1:3

PSALM 113:1-4
Laudate, pueri

1   Praise the LORD. Sing praises, you servants of the LORD; *
      O praise the Name of the LORD.
2   Blessed be the Name of the LORD, *
      from this time forth for evermore.
3   The LORD's Name be praised *
      from the rising up of the sun to the going down
      of the same.
4   The LORD is high above all nations, *
      and his glory above the heavens.

Glory be to the Father, and to the Son, and to the Holy Spirit: *
   as it was in the beginning, is now, and ever shall be,
   world without end. Amen.

A READING FROM HOLY SCRIPTURE

Abide in me, and I in you. As the branch cannot bear fruit by itself, unless it abides in the vine, neither can you, unless you abide in me. I am the vine; you are the branches. Whoever abides in me and I in him, he it is that bears much fruit, for apart from me you can do nothing.   JOHN 15:4-5

or this

Do not be anxious about anything, but in everything by prayer and supplication with thanksgiving let your requests be made known to God. And the peace of God, which surpasses all understanding, will guard your hearts and your minds in Christ Jesus.   PHILIPPIANS 4:6-7

A period of silence may follow.

Prayers may be offered for ourselves and others.

THE LORD'S PRAYER

THE COLLECT

Blessed Savior, at this hour you hung upon the Cross, stretching out your loving arms: Grant that all the peoples of the earth may look to you and be saved; for your tender mercies' sake. **Amen.**

IN THE EARLY EVENING

This devotion may be used before or after the evening meal.

The following or some other verse of Scripture is said

How excellent is your mercy, O God!
    The children of men shall take refuge under the shadow
    of your wings.
For with you is the well of life,
    and in your light shall we see light.   PSALM 36:7, 9

PHOS HILARON
O Gladsome Light

O gladsome light,
pure brightness of the everliving Father in heaven, *
    O Jesus Christ, holy and blessed!
Now as we come to the setting of the sun,
and our eyes behold the vesper light, *
    we sing your praises, O God: Father, Son, and Holy Spirit.
You are worthy at all times to be praised by happy voices, *
    O Son of God, O Giver of Life,
    and to be glorified through all the worlds.

A READING FROM HOLY SCRIPTURE

For what we proclaim is not ourselves, but Jesus Christ as Lord, with ourselves as your servants for Jesus' sake. For God, who said, "Let light shine out of darkness," has shone in our hearts, to give the light of the knowledge of the glory of God in the face of Jesus Christ.   2 CORINTHIANS 4:5-6

or this

Jesus spoke to them, saying, "I am the light of the world. Whoever follows me will not walk in darkness, but will have the light of life." JOHN 8:12

or this

Jesus said, "Behold, I stand at the door and knock. If anyone hears my voice and opens the door, I will come in to him and eat with him, and he with me." REVELATION 3:20

A period of silence may follow.

A hymn or canticle may be used; the Apostles' Creed (page 75) may be said.

Prayers may be offered for ourselves and others.

THE LORD'S PRAYER

THE COLLECT

Lord Jesus, stay with us, for evening is at hand and the day is past; be our companion in the way, kindle our hearts, and awaken hope, that we may know you as you are revealed in Scripture and the breaking of bread. Grant this for the sake of your love. **Amen.**

AT THE CLOSE OF DAY

The following or some other verse of Scripture is said

I will lay me down in peace, and take my rest;
for you, LORD, only, make me dwell in safety.   PSALM 4:8

PSALM 134
Ecce nunc

1 Behold now, praise the LORD, *
    all you servants of the LORD,
2 You that stand by night in the house of the LORD, *
    even in the courts of the house of our God.
3 Lift up your hands in the sanctuary *
    and sing praises unto the LORD.
4 The LORD who made heaven and earth *
    give you blessing out of Zion.

A READING FROM HOLY SCRIPTURE

You keep them in perfect peace whose minds are stayed on you,
because they trust in you. Trust in the LORD for ever, for the
LORD God is an everlasting rock.   ISAIAH 26:3-4ᵀ

or this

Now may the God of peace himself sanctify you completely,
and may your whole spirit and soul and body be kept blameless
at the coming of our Lord Jesus Christ.   1 THESSALONIANS 5:23

A period of silence may follow.

A hymn or canticle may be used.

*Prayers may be offered for ourselves and others. It is appropriate that prayers of
thanksgiving for the blessings of the day, and penitence for our sins, be included.*

THE COLLECT

Visit this place, O Lord, and drive far from it all snares of the enemy; let your holy angels dwell with us to preserve us in peace; and let your blessing be upon us always; through Jesus Christ our Lord. **Amen.**

NUNC DIMITTIS
The Song of Simeon

Lord, now let your servant depart in peace, *
    according to your word.
For my eyes have seen your salvation, *
    which you have prepared before the face of all people;
To be a light to lighten the Gentiles, *
    and to be the glory of your people Israel.

Glory be to the Father, and to the Son, and to the Holy Spirit; *
    as it was in the beginning, is now, and ever shall be,
    world without end. Amen.
                              LUKE 2:29-32

CONCLUDING SENTENCE

The almighty and merciful Lord, Father, Son, and Holy Spirit, bless us and keep us, this night and evermore. **Amen.**

When the Apostles Creed is included in Family Prayer, the text is as follows:

THE APOSTLES' CREED

I believe in God, the Father almighty,
    creator of heaven and earth.
I believe in Jesus Christ, his only Son, our Lord.
    He was conceived by the Holy Spirit
    and born of the Virgin Mary.
    He suffered under Pontius Pilate,
    was crucified, died, and was buried.
    He descended to the dead.
    On the third day he rose again.
    He ascended into heaven,
    and is seated at the right hand of the Father.
    He will come again to judge the living and the dead.
I believe in the Holy Spirit,
    the holy catholic Church,
    the communion of saints,
    the forgiveness of sins,
    the resurrection of the body,
    and the life everlasting. Amen.

ADDITIONAL PRAYERS

FOR THE SPIRIT OF PRAYER

O Almighty God, you pour out on all who desire it the spirit of grace and of supplication: Deliver us, when we draw near to you, from coldness of heart and wanderings of mind, that with steadfast thoughts and kindled affections we may worship you in spirit and in truth; through Jesus Christ our Lord. **Amen.**

FOR THOSE WE LOVE

Almighty God, we entrust all who are dear to us to your never-failing care and love, for this life and the life to come, knowing that you are doing for them better things than we can desire or pray for; through Jesus Christ our Lord. **Amen.**

FOR THE FAMILY

Merciful Savior, you loved Martha and Mary and Lazarus, hallowing their home with your sacred presence: Bless our home, we pray, that your love may rest upon us, and that your presence may dwell with us. May we all grow in grace and in the knowledge of you, our Lord and Savior. Teach us to love one another as you have commanded. Help us to bear one another's burdens in fulfillment of your law, O blessed Jesus, who with the Father and the Holy Spirit live and reign, one God, for ever and ever. **Amen.**

FOR RELATIVES AND FRIENDS

O Loving Father, we commend to your gracious keeping all who are near and dear to us. Have mercy upon any who are sick, and comfort those who are in pain, anxiety, or sorrow. Awaken all who are careless about eternal things. Bless those who are young and in health, that they may give the days of their strength to you. Comfort the aged and infirm, that your peace may rest upon them. Hallow the ties of kindred, that we may help and not hinder one another in all the good works that you have prepared for us to walk in; through Jesus Christ our Lord. **Amen.**

FOR CHILDREN

O Lord Jesus Christ, who took little children into your arms and blessed them: Bless the children of this family, that they may grow up in godly fear and love. Give them your strength and guidance day by day, that they may continue in your love and service to their lives' end. Grant this, O blessed Savior, for your own Name's sake. **Amen.**

IN THE MORNING

O God, the King eternal, whose light divides the day from the night and turns the shadow of death into the morning: Drive far from us all wrong desires, incline our hearts to keep your law, and guide our feet into the way of peace; that, having done your will with cheerfulness during the day, we may, when night comes, rejoice to give you thanks; through Jesus Christ our Lord. **Amen.**

AT NIGHT

O Lord, support us all the day long through this trouble-filled life, until the shadows lengthen, and the evening comes, and the busy world is hushed, and the fever of life is over, and our work is done. Then in your mercy grant us a safe lodging, and a holy rest, and peace at the last. **Amen.**

O God of peace, who hast taught us that in returning and rest we shall be saved, in quietness and in confidence shall be our strength: By the might of thy Spirit lift us, we pray thee, to thy presence, where we may be still and know that thou art God; through Jesus Christ our Lord. **Amen.**

FAMILY RESPONSES BEFORE MEALS
Traditional

The eyes of all wait upon thee, O Lord;
  And thou givest them their meat in due season.
Thou openest thine hand;
  And fillest all things living with plenteousness.
Bless us, O Lord, and these thy gifts, which we are about to receive from thy bounty, through Christ our Lord. **Amen.**

A GRACE BEFORE MEALS

Bless, O Lord, these gifts to our use, and us to your service, and make us ever mindful of the needs of others, through Jesus Christ our Lord. **Amen.**

ADVENT ANTIPHONS

In Advent, using the Antiphons found in the Calendar of Holy Days and Commemorations (page 712), families might consider singing the appropriate verse of the hymn "O Come, O Come, Emmanuel" each night beginning on December 16.

THE GREAT LITANY

To be said or sung, kneeling, standing, or in procession.

O God the Father, Creator of heaven and earth,
Have mercy upon us.

O God the Son, Redeemer of the world,
Have mercy upon us.

O God the Holy Spirit, Sanctifier of the faithful,
Have mercy upon us.

O holy, blessed, and glorious Trinity, one God,
Have mercy upon us.

Remember not, Lord Jesus, our offenses, nor the offenses of
our forebears; neither reward us according to our sins. Spare us,
good Lord, spare your people, whom you have redeemed with
your most precious blood, and by your mercy preserve us for ever.
Spare us, good Lord.

From all evil and wickedness; from sin; from the works and assaults
of the devil; from your wrath and everlasting condemnation,
Good Lord, deliver us.

From all blindness of heart; from pride, vanity, and hypocrisy;
from envy, hatred, and malice; and from all lack of charity,
Good Lord, deliver us.

From all disordered and sinful affections; and from all the deceits of the world, the flesh, and the devil,
Good Lord, deliver us.

From all false doctrine, heresy, and schism; from hardness of heart, and contempt of your Word and commandments,
Good Lord, deliver us.

From lightning and tempest; from earthquake, fire, and flood; from plague, pestilence, and famine,
Good Lord, deliver us.

From all oppression, conspiracy, and rebellion; from violence, battle, and murder; and from dying suddenly and unprepared,
Good Lord, deliver us.

By the mystery of your holy incarnation; by your holy nativity and submission to the Law; by your baptism, fasting, and temptation,
Good Lord, deliver us.

By your agony and bloody sweat; by your Cross and passion; by your precious death and burial,
Good Lord, deliver us.

By your glorious resurrection and ascension; by the sending of the Holy Spirit; by your heavenly intercession; and by your coming again in power and great glory,
Good Lord, deliver us.

In all times of tribulation; in all times of prosperity; in the hour of death, and in the day of judgment,
Good Lord, deliver us.

We sinners beseech you to hear us, O Lord God: That it may please you to rule and govern your holy Church universal in the right way,
We beseech you to hear us, good Lord.

To illumine all Bishops, Priests, and Deacons, with true knowledge and understanding of your Word; and that, both by their preaching and living, they may show it accordingly,
We beseech you to hear us, good Lord.

To send forth laborers into your harvest; to prosper their work by your Holy Spirit; to make your saving health known unto all nations; and to hasten the coming of your kingdom,
We beseech you to hear us, good Lord.

To give all your people increase of grace to hear your Word with humility, to receive it with pure affection, and to bring forth the fruit of the Spirit,
We beseech you to hear us, good Lord.

To bring into the way of truth all who have erred and are deceived,
We beseech you to hear us, good Lord.

To give us a heart to love and fear you, and diligently to keep your commandments,
We beseech you to hear us, good Lord.

To bless and keep all your people,
We beseech you to hear us, good Lord.

That it may please you to rule the hearts of your servant *N*, the *President/Sovereign/Prime Minister*, and all others in authority, that they may do justice, and show mercy, and walk humbly before you,
We beseech you to hear us, good Lord.

To bless and guide all judges, giving them grace to execute justice, and to maintain truth,
We beseech you to hear us, good Lord.

To bless and keep our armed forces by sea, and land, and air, and to shield them in all dangers and adversities,
We beseech you to hear us, good Lord.

To bless and protect all who serve their communities by their labor and learning,
We beseech you to hear us, good Lord.

To give and preserve for us and for others the bountiful fruits of the earth, so that at the harvest we all may enjoy them,
We beseech you to hear us, good Lord.

To make wars to cease in all the world, and to give to all nations unity, peace, and concord,
We beseech you to hear us, good Lord.

That it may please you to show mercy on all prisoners and captives; refugees, the homeless, and the hungry; and all those who are desolate and oppressed,
We beseech you to hear us, good Lord.

To preserve all who are in danger by reason of their work or travel,
We beseech you to hear us, good Lord.

To strengthen the bonds of those in Holy Matrimony; to uphold the widowed and abandoned; and to comfort all whose homes are torn by strife,
We beseech you to hear us, good Lord.

To protect the unborn and their parents, and to preserve all women in childbirth;
We beseech you to hear us, good Lord.

To care for those who have lost children or face infertility, and to provide for young children and orphans,
We beseech you to hear us, good Lord.

To visit the lonely and those who grieve; to strengthen all who suffer in mind, body, or spirit; and to comfort with your presence those who are failing and infirm,
We beseech you to hear us, good Lord.

To support, help, and deliver all who are in danger, necessity, and tribulation,
We beseech you to hear us, good Lord.

To have mercy upon all people,
We beseech you to hear us, good Lord.

That it may please you to give us true repentance; to forgive us all our sin, negligence, and ignorance; and to endue us with the grace of your Holy Spirit to amend our lives according to your holy Word,
We beseech you to hear us, good Lord.

To forgive our enemies, persecutors, and slanderers, and to turn their hearts,
We beseech you to hear us, good Lord.

To strengthen those who stand; to encourage the faint-hearted; to raise up those who fall; and finally to beat down Satan under our feet,
We beseech you to hear us, good Lord.

To grant to all the faithful departed eternal life and peace,
We beseech you to hear us, good Lord.

To grant that, in the fellowship of [_____ and] all the saints, we may attain to your heavenly kingdom,
We beseech you to hear us, good Lord.

Son of God, we beseech you to hear us.
Son of God, we beseech you to hear us.

O Lamb of God, you take away the sin of the world;
Have mercy upon us.

O Lamb of God, you take away the sin of the world;
Have mercy upon us.

O Lamb of God, you take away the sin of the world;
Grant us your peace.

O Christ, hear us.
O Christ, hear us.

Lord, have mercy upon us.
Christ, have mercy upon us.
Lord, have mercy upon us.

When the Litany is sung or said immediately before the Eucharist, the Litany concludes here, and the Eucharist begins with the Salutation ("The Lord be with you") and the Collect of the Day.

On all other occasions, the Officiant and People say or sing together

Our Father, who art in heaven,	Our Father in heaven,
hallowed be thy Name,	hallowed be your Name,
thy kingdom come,	your kingdom come,
thy will be done,	your will be done,
on earth as it is in heaven.	on earth as it is in heaven.
Give us this day our daily bread.	Give us today our daily bread.
And forgive us our trespasses,	And forgive us our sins
as we forgive those	as we forgive those
who trespass against us.	who sin against us.
And lead us not into temptation,	Save us from the time of trial,
but deliver us from evil.	and deliver us from evil.
For thine is the kingdom,	For the kingdom, the power,
and the power, and the glory,	and the glory are yours,
for ever and ever. Amen.	now and for ever. Amen.

O Lord, show us your love and mercy;
  For we have put our trust in you.

The Officiant says the following

Almighty God, you have promised to hear the petitions of those
who ask in the Name of your Son: Mercifully incline your ear
to us who have made our prayers and supplications to you; and
grant that what we have asked faithfully, according to your will,
we may obtain effectually, for the relief of our necessities and the
setting forth of your glory; through Jesus Christ our Lord. **Amen.**

The Officiant may add other prayers, and may end the Litany, saying

The grace of our Lord Jesus Christ, and the love of God, and the
fellowship of the Holy Spirit, be with us all evermore. **Amen.**

THE SUPPLICATION

*For use in the Litany in place of the Versicle and Collect which follows the Lord's
Prayer; or at the end of Morning or Evening Prayer; or as a separate devotion.
The Supplication is especially appropriate in times of war, or of great anxiety, or
of disaster.*

O Lord, arise and help us;
  And deliver us for your Name's sake.

O God, we have heard with our ears, and our forebears have
declared to us, the noble works that you did in their days, and in
the time before them.

O Lord, arise and help us;
  And deliver us for your Name's sake.

Glory be to the Father, and to the Son, and to the Holy Spirit;
as it was in the beginning, is now, and ever shall be,
world without end. **Amen.**

O Lord, arise and help us;
And deliver us for your Name's sake.

From our enemies defend us, O Christ;
Graciously behold our afflictions.

With pity behold the sorrows of our hearts;
Mercifully forgive the sins of your people.

With favor hear our prayers;
O Son of David, have mercy upon us.

Be pleased to hear us, O Christ;
**Graciously hear us, O Christ; graciously hear us,
O Lord Christ.**

The Officiant prays

Let us pray.

Look mercifully, O Father, on our infirmities; and, for the glory of your Name, rescue us from all those evils we now endure; and grant that in all our troubles we may put our whole trust and confidence in your mercy, serving you in holiness and purity of life, to your honor and glory; through our only Mediator and Advocate, Jesus Christ our Lord. **Amen.**

The Supplication may end here, or may conclude with the prayer of St. John Chrysostom and the Grace (page 52).

ADDITIONAL DIRECTIONS

The Great Litany may be used before the Eucharist, after the Collects of Morning or Evening Prayer, or separately.

It is particularly appropriate to use the Great Litany on the First Sunday of Advent and the First Sunday in Lent. It is also appropriate for Rogation days, other days of fasting or thanksgiving, and occasions of solemn and comprehensive entreaty.

Where local circumstance or pastoral need dictates, the Officiant may reduce the number of petitions and responses prayed.

THE DECALOGUE

Celebrant God spoke these words and said:
I am the LORD your God.
You shall have no other gods but me.

People **Lord, have mercy upon us,
and incline our hearts to keep this law.**

Celebrant You shall not make for yourself any idol.

People **Lord, have mercy upon us,
and incline our hearts to keep this law.**

Celebrant You shall not take the Name of the LORD your God
in vain.

People **Lord, have mercy upon us,
and incline our hearts to keep this law.**

Celebrant Remember the Sabbath day and keep it holy.

People **Lord, have mercy upon us,
and incline our hearts to keep this law.**

Celebrant Honor your father and your mother.

People **Lord, have mercy upon us,
and incline our hearts to keep this law.**

Celebrant You shall not murder.

People **Lord, have mercy upon us,
and incline our hearts to keep this law.**

Celebrant You shall not commit adultery.
People Lord, have mercy upon us,
   and incline our hearts to keep this law.

Celebrant You shall not steal.
People Lord, have mercy upon us,
   and incline our hearts to keep this law.

Celebrant You shall not bear false witness against your neighbor.
People Lord, have mercy upon us,
   and incline our hearts to keep this law.

Celebrant You shall not covet.
People Lord, have mercy upon us,
   and write all these, your laws,
   in our hearts, we beseech you.

EXODUS 20:1-17[T]; DEUTERONOMY 5:6-21[T]

79

CONCERNING THE HOLY EUCHARIST

Holy Communion is normally the principal service of Christian worship on the Lord's Day, and on other appointed Feasts and Holy Days. Two forms of the liturgy, commonly called the Lord's Supper or the Holy Eucharist, are provided.

The Anglican Standard Text is essentially that of the Holy Communion service of the *Book of Common Prayer* of 1662 and successor books through 1928 and 1962. The Anglican Standard Text is presented in contemporary English and in the order for Holy Communion that is common, since the late twentieth century, among ecumenical and Anglican partners worldwide. The Anglican Standard Text may be conformed to its original content and ordering, as in the 1662 or subsequent books; the Additional Directions give clear guidance on how this is to be accomplished. Similarly, there are directions given as to how the Anglican Standard Text may be abbreviated where appropriate for local mission and ministry.

The Renewed Ancient Text is drawn from liturgies of the Early Church, reflects the influence of twentieth century ecumenical consensus, and includes elements of historic Anglican piety.

A comprehensive collection of Additional Directions concerning Holy Communion is found after the Renewed Ancient Text.

THE LORD'S SUPPER
or
HOLY COMMUNION,
COMMONLY CALLED
THE HOLY EUCHARIST
Anglican Standard Text

A hymn, psalm, or anthem may be sung.

THE ACCLAMATION

The People standing, the Celebrant says this or a seasonal greeting (pages 145-146)

Blessed be God: the Father, the Son, and the Holy Spirit.

People **And blessed be his kingdom, now and for ever. Amen.**

In the season of Lent

Celebrant Bless the Lord who forgives all our sins.

People **His mercy endures for ever.**

From Easter Day until the Eve of Pentecost

Celebrant Alleluia! Christ is risen!

People **The Lord is risen indeed! Alleluia!**

THE COLLECT FOR PURITY

The Celebrant prays (and the People may be invited to join)

Almighty God, to you all hearts are open, all desires known, and from you no secrets are hid: Cleanse the thoughts of our hearts by the inspiration of your Holy Spirit, that we may perfectly love you, and worthily magnify your holy Name; through Christ our Lord. **Amen.**

THE SUMMARY OF THE LAW

Then follows the Summary of the Law, or The Decalogue (page 100).

Hear what our Lord Jesus Christ says:
You shall love the Lord your God with all your heart and with all your soul and with all your mind. This is the first and great commandment. And the second is like it: You shall love your neighbor as yourself. On these two commandments depend all the Law and the Prophets.   MATTHEW 22:37-40[T]

THE KYRIE

The Celebrant and People pray

Lord, have mercy upon us.	Lord, have mercy.	Kyrie eleison.
Christ, have mercy upon us.	*or* **Christ, have mercy.**	*or* **Christe eleison.**
Lord, have mercy upon us.	Lord, have mercy.	Kyrie eleison.

or this

THE TRISAGION

Holy God,
Holy and Mighty,
Holy Immortal One,
Have mercy upon us.

The Gloria or some other song of praise may be sung or said, all standing. It is appropriate to omit the song of praise during penitential seasons and days appointed for fasting.

Glory to God in the highest,
   and peace to his people on earth.
Lord God, heavenly King,
almighty God and Father,
   we worship you, we give you thanks,
   we praise you for your glory.
Lord Jesus Christ, only Son of the Father,
Lord God, Lamb of God,
you take away the sin of the world:
   have mercy on us;
you are seated at the right hand of the Father:
   receive our prayer.
For you alone are the Holy One,
you alone are the Lord,
you alone are the Most High,
   Jesus Christ,
   with the Holy Spirit,
   in the glory of God the Father. Amen.

THE COLLECT OF THE DAY

The Celebrant says to the People

     The Lord be with you.
People **And with your spirit.**
Celebrant Let us pray.

The Celebrant prays the Collect.

People **Amen.**

One or more Lessons, as appointed, are read, the Reader first saying

A Reading from _____.

A citation giving chapter and verse may be added.

After each Lesson the Reader may say

The Word of the Lord.
People **Thanks be to God.**

Or the Reader may say Here ends the Reading.

Silence may follow.

A psalm, hymn, or anthem may follow each reading.

All standing, the Deacon or Priest reads the Gospel, first saying

The Holy Gospel of our Lord Jesus Christ according to _____.

People **Glory to you, Lord Christ.**

After the Gospel, the Reader says

The Gospel of the Lord.
People **Praise to you, Lord Christ.**

THE SERMON

THE NICENE CREED

On Sundays, other Major Feast Days, and other times as appointed, all stand to recite the Nicene Creed, the Celebrant first saying

Let us confess our faith in the words of the Nicene Creed:

We believe in one God,
    the Father, the Almighty,
    maker of heaven and earth,
    of all that is, visible and invisible.

We believe in one Lord, Jesus Christ,
    the only-begotten Son of God,
    eternally begotten of the Father,
    God from God, Light from Light,
    true God from true God,
    begotten, not made,
    of one Being with the Father;
    through him all things were made.
    For us and for our salvation he came down from heaven,
    was incarnate from the Holy Spirit and the Virgin Mary,
    and was made man.
    For our sake he was crucified under Pontius Pilate;
    he suffered death and was buried.
    On the third day he rose again in accordance with the Scriptures;
    he ascended into heaven
    and is seated at the right hand of the Father.
    He will come again in glory to judge the living and the dead,
    and his kingdom will have no end.

We believe in the Holy Spirit, the Lord, the giver of life,
    who proceeds from the Father [and the Son],[†]
    who with the Father and the Son is worshiped and glorified,
    who has spoken through the prophets.
    We believe in one holy catholic and apostolic Church.
    We acknowledge one Baptism for the forgiveness of sins.
    We look for the resurrection of the dead,
    and the life of the world to come. Amen.

† *The phrase "and the Son" (Latin* filioque*) is not in the original Greek text. See the resolution of the College of Bishops concerning the filioque in Documentary Foundations (page 768).*

The Deacon or other person appointed says these prayers, or the Prayers of the People in the Renewed Ancient Text.

Let us pray for the Church and for the world.

Almighty and everliving God, we are taught by your holy Word to offer prayers and supplications and to give thanks for all people. We humbly ask you mercifully to receive our prayers. Inspire continually the universal Church with the spirit of truth, unity, and concord; and grant that all who confess your holy Name may agree in the truth of your holy Word, and live in unity and godly love.

Silence

> *Reader* Lord, in your mercy:
> *People* **Hear our prayer.**

We pray that you will lead the nations of the world in the way of righteousness; and so guide and direct their leaders, especially *N, our President/Sovereign/Prime Minister*, that your people may enjoy the blessings of freedom and peace. Grant that our leaders may impartially administer justice, uphold integrity and truth, restrain wickedness and vice, and protect true religion and virtue.

Silence

> *Reader* Lord, in your mercy:
> *People* **Hear our prayer.**

Give grace, heavenly Father, to all Bishops, Priests, and Deacons, *and especially to your servant(s) N, our Archbishop/Bishop/Priest/ Deacon, etc.*, that by their life and teaching, they may proclaim your true and life-giving Word, and rightly and duly administer your holy Sacraments. And to all your people give your heavenly grace, especially to this Congregation, that with reverent and obedient hearts we may hear and receive your holy Word, and serve you in holiness and righteousness all the days of our lives.

Silence

> *Reader*   Lord, in your mercy:
> *People*   **Hear our prayer.**

Prosper, we pray, all those who proclaim the Gospel of your kingdom throughout the world, and strengthen us to fulfill your great commission, making disciples of all nations, baptizing them and teaching them to obey all that you have commanded.

Silence

> *Reader*   Lord, in your mercy:
> *People*   **Hear our prayer.**

We ask you in your goodness, O Lord, to comfort and sustain all who in this transitory life are in trouble, sorrow, need, sickness, or any other adversity [especially _____].

Silence

> *Reader*   Lord, in your mercy:
> *People*   **Hear our prayer.**

We remember before you all your servants who have departed this life in your faith and fear, [especially _____,] that your will for them may be fulfilled; and we ask you to give us grace to follow the good examples of [*N.*, and] all your saints, that we may share with them in your heavenly kingdom.

Silence

Additional prayers may be added.

The Celebrant concludes with this or some other appropriate Collect.

Heavenly Father, grant these our prayers for the sake of Jesus
Christ, our only Mediator and Advocate, who lives and reigns
with you in the unity of the Holy Spirit, one God, now and for
ever. **Amen.**

The Celebrant may then say the Exhortation.

THE CONFESSION AND ABSOLUTION OF SIN

The Deacon or other person appointed says the following

All who truly and earnestly repent of your sins, and seek to live
in love and charity with your neighbors, and intend to lead the
new life, following the commandments of God, and walking
in his holy ways: draw near with faith and make your humble
confession to Almighty God.

or

Let us humbly confess our sins to Almighty God.

Silence

The Deacon and People kneel as able and pray

**Almighty God, Father of our Lord Jesus Christ,
    maker and judge of us all:
We acknowledge and lament our many sins and offenses,
    which we have committed by thought, word, and deed**

against your divine majesty,
   provoking most justly your righteous anger against us.
We are deeply sorry for these our transgressions;
   the burden of them is more than we can bear.
Have mercy upon us,
Have mercy upon us, most merciful Father;
   for your Son our Lord Jesus Christ's sake,
   forgive us all that is past;
   and grant that we may evermore serve and please you in
   newness of life,
   to the honor and glory of your Name;
   through Jesus Christ our Lord. Amen.

The Bishop or Priest stands and says

Almighty God, our heavenly Father, who in his great mercy has
promised forgiveness of sins to all those who sincerely repent
and with true faith turn to him, have mercy upon you, pardon
and deliver you from all your sins, confirm and strengthen you
in all goodness, and bring you to everlasting life; through Jesus
Christ our Lord. **Amen.**

THE COMFORTABLE WORDS

The Celebrant may then say one or more of the following sentences, first saying

Hear the Word of God to all who truly turn to him.

Come to me, all who labor and are heavy laden, and I will give
you rest.   MATTHEW 11:28

God so loved the world, that he gave his only-begotten Son,
that whoever believes in him should not perish but have eternal
life.   JOHN 3:16ᵀ

The saying is trustworthy and deserving of full
acceptance, that Christ Jesus came into the world to
save sinners. 1 TIMOTHY 1:15

If anyone sins, we have an advocate with the Father, Jesus Christ
the righteous. He is the propitiation for our sins, and not for
ours only, but also for the sins of the whole world. 1 JOHN 2:1-2ᵀ

THE PEACE

Celebrant	The Peace of the Lord be always with you.
People	**And with your spirit.**

Then the Ministers and People may greet one another in the Name of the Lord.

THE OFFERTORY

The Celebrant may begin the Offertory with one of the provided sentences of Scripture.

*During the Offertory a hymn, psalm, or anthem may be sung. The Deacon
or Priest prepares the Holy Table for the celebration. Representatives of the
Congregation may bring the People's offerings of bread and wine, and money or
other gifts, to the Deacon or Priest.*

The People stand while the offerings are presented. The following may be said.

Celebrant	Yours, O LORD, is the greatness, and the power, and the glory, and the victory, and the majesty: for everything in heaven and on earth is yours; yours is the kingdom, O LORD, and you are exalted as Head above all. All things come from you, O LORD,
People	**And of your own have we given you.**

1 CHRONICLES 29:11, 14ᵀ

The People remain standing. The Celebrant faces them and sings or says

	The Lord be with you.
People	**And with your spirit.**
Celebrant	Lift up your hearts.
People	**We lift them up to the Lord.**
Celebrant	Let us give thanks to the Lord our God.
People	**It is right to give him thanks and praise.**

The Celebrant continues

It is right, our duty and our joy, always and everywhere to give thanks to you, Father Almighty, Creator of heaven and earth.

Here a Proper Preface (pages 152-158) is normally sung or said.

Therefore we praise you, joining our voices with Angels and Archangels and with all the company of heaven, who for ever sing this hymn to proclaim the glory of your Name:

THE SANCTUS

Celebrant and People

Holy, Holy, Holy, Lord God of power and might, heaven and
    earth are full of your glory.
    Hosanna in the highest.
Blessed is he who comes in the Name of the Lord.
    Hosanna in the highest.

THE PRAYER OF CONSECRATION

The People kneel or stand. The Celebrant continues

All praise and glory is yours, O God our heavenly Father, for in your tender mercy, you gave your only Son Jesus Christ to suffer death upon the Cross for our redemption. He made there, by his one oblation of himself once offered, a full, perfect, and sufficient sacrifice, oblation, and satisfaction, for the sins of the whole world; and he instituted, and in his Holy Gospel commanded us to continue, a perpetual memory of his precious death and sacrifice, until his coming again.

So now, O merciful Father, in your great goodness, we ask you to bless and sanctify, with your Word and Holy Spirit, these gifts of bread and wine, that we, receiving them according to your Son our Savior Jesus Christ's holy institution, in remembrance of his death and passion, may be partakers of his most blessed Body and Blood. [†]

At the following words concerning the bread, the Celebrant is to hold it, or lay a hand upon it, and here* may break the bread; and at the words concerning the cup, to hold or place a hand upon the cup and any other vessel containing the wine to be consecrated.

For on the night that he was betrayed, our Lord Jesus Christ took bread; and when he had given thanks, he broke it,* and gave it to his disciples, saying, "Take, eat; this is my Body, which is given for you: Do this in remembrance of me."

Likewise, after supper, Jesus took the cup, and when he had given thanks, he gave it to them, saying, "Drink this, all of you; for this is my Blood of the New Covenant, which is shed for you, and for many, for the forgiveness of sins: Whenever you drink it, do this in remembrance of me." [‡]

[†] *This paragraph does not occur in the 1662 Book of Common Prayer, but ecumenical consensus expects its use.*

[‡] *In the 1662 Order, the Distribution of Communion occurs here. The Lord's Prayer is then said. The remainder of the Prayer of Consecration follows the Lord's Prayer as an alternative Post Communion Prayer.*

Therefore, O Lord and heavenly Father, according to the institution of your dearly beloved Son our Savior Jesus Christ, we your humble servants celebrate and make here before your divine Majesty, with these holy gifts, the memorial your Son commanded us to make; remembering his blessed passion and precious death, his mighty resurrection and glorious ascension, and his promise to come again.

And we earnestly desire your fatherly goodness mercifully to accept this, our sacrifice of praise and thanksgiving; asking you to grant that, by the merits and death of your Son Jesus Christ, and through faith in his Blood, we and your whole Church may obtain forgiveness of our sins, and all other benefits of his passion.

And here we offer and present to you, O Lord, ourselves, our souls and bodies, to be a reasonable, holy, and living sacrifice. We humbly pray that all who partake of this Holy Communion may worthily receive the most precious Body and Blood of your Son Jesus Christ, be filled with your grace and heavenly benediction, and be made one body with him, that he may dwell in us, and we in him.

And although we are unworthy, because of our many sins, to offer you any sacrifice, yet we ask you to accept this duty and service we owe, not weighing our merits, but pardoning our offenses, through Jesus Christ our Lord.

By him, and with him, and in him, in the unity of the Holy Spirit, all honor and glory is yours, Almighty Father, now and for ever. **Amen.**

The Celebrant then says

And now as our Savior Christ has taught us, we are bold to pray:

Celebrant and People together pray

Our Father, who art in heaven,
    hallowed be thy Name,
    thy kingdom come,
    thy will be done,
    on earth as it is in heaven.
Give us this day our daily bread.
And forgive us our trespasses,
    as we forgive those
    who trespass against us.
And lead us not into temptation,
    but deliver us from evil.
For thine is the kingdom,
    and the power, and the glory,
    for ever and ever. Amen.
	Our Father in heaven,
	    hallowed be your Name,
	    your kingdom come,
	    your will be done,
	    on earth as it is in heaven.
	Give us today our daily bread.
	And forgive us our sins
	    as we forgive those
	    who sin against us.
	Save us from the time of trial,
	    and deliver us from evil.
	For the kingdom, the power,
	    and the glory are yours,
	    now and for ever. Amen.

THE FRACTION

If the consecrated Bread was not broken earlier, the Celebrant breaks it now.
A period of silence is kept.

Then may be sung or said

Celebrant	[Alleluia.] Christ our Passover is sacrificed for us.
People	**Therefore let us keep the feast. [Alleluia.]**

or this

Celebrant	[Alleluia.] Christ our Passover Lamb has been sacrificed, once for all upon the Cross.
People	**Therefore let us keep the feast. [Alleluia.]**

In Lent, Alleluia is omitted, and may be omitted at other times except during Easter Season.

THE PRAYER OF HUMBLE ACCESS

Celebrant and People together may say

We do not presume to come to this your table, O merciful Lord,
    trusting in our own righteousness,
    but in your abundant and great mercies.
We are not worthy so much as to gather up
    the crumbs under your table;
    but you are the same Lord
    whose character is always to have mercy.
Grant us, therefore, gracious Lord,
    so to eat the flesh of your dear Son Jesus Christ,
    and to drink his blood,
    that our sinful bodies may be made clean by his body,
    and our souls washed through his most precious blood,
    and that we may evermore dwell in him, and he in us. Amen.

THE AGNUS DEI

The following or some other suitable anthem may be sung or said here

Lamb of God, you take away the sin of the world;
    have mercy on us.
Lamb of God, you take away the sin of the world;
    have mercy on us.
Lamb of God, you take away the sin of the world;
    grant us your peace.

THE MINISTRATION OF COMMUNION

Facing the People, the Celebrant may say the following invitation

The gifts of God for the people of God. [Take them in remembrance that Christ died for you and feed on him in your hearts by faith, with thanksgiving.]

or this

Behold the Lamb of God, behold him who takes away the sins of the world. Blessed are those who are invited to the marriage supper of the Lamb. JOHN 1:29ᵀ, REVELATION 19:9

The Ministers receive the Sacrament in both kinds, and then immediately deliver it to the People.

The Bread and Cup are given to the communicants with these words

The Body of our Lord Jesus Christ, [which was given for you, preserve your body and soul to everlasting life. Take and eat this in remembrance that Christ died for you, and feed on him in your heart by faith, with thanksgiving.]

The Blood of our Lord Jesus Christ, [which was shed for you, preserve your body and soul to everlasting life. Drink this in remembrance that Christ's Blood was shed for you, and be thankful.]

During the ministration of Communion, hymns, psalms, or anthems may be sung.

The Celebrant may offer a sentence of Scripture at the conclusion of the Communion.

THE POST COMMUNION PRAYER

After Communion, the Celebrant says

Let us pray.

Celebrant and People together say the following, or the Post Communion Prayer in the Renewed Ancient Text

Almighty and everliving God,
we thank you for feeding us, in these holy mysteries,
　with the spiritual food of the most precious Body and Blood
　of your Son our Savior Jesus Christ;
and for assuring us, through this Sacrament, of your favor and
　goodness towards us:
　　that we are true members of the mystical body of your Son,
　　the blessed company of all faithful people;
　　and are also heirs, through hope,
　　of your everlasting kingdom.
And we humbly ask you, heavenly Father,
　to assist us with your grace,
　　that we may continue in that holy fellowship,
　　and do all the good works that you have prepared for us to
　　walk in;
through Jesus Christ our Lord,
　to whom, with you and the Holy Spirit,
　be all honor and glory, now and for ever. Amen.

THE BLESSING

The Bishop when present, or the Priest, gives this or an alternate blessing

The peace of God, which passes all understanding, keep your
hearts and minds in the knowledge and love of God, and of his
Son Jesus Christ our Lord; and the blessing of God Almighty,
the Father, the Son, and the Holy Spirit, be among you, and
remain with you always. **Amen.**

A hymn, psalm, or anthem may be sung after the Blessing (or following the Dismissal).

The Deacon, or the Priest, may dismiss the People with these words

Let us go forth in the Name of Christ.

People **Thanks be to God.**

or this

Deacon Go in peace to love and serve the Lord.

People **Thanks be to God.**

or this

Deacon Let us go forth into the world, rejoicing in the power of the Holy Spirit.

People **Thanks be to God.**

or this

Deacon Let us bless the Lord.

People **Thanks be to God.**

From the Easter Vigil through the Day of Pentecost, "Alleluia, alleluia" is added to any of the dismissals. It may be added at other times, except during Lent and on other penitential occasions.

The People respond

Thanks be to God. Alleluia, alleluia.

THE LORD'S SUPPER

or

HOLY COMMUNION,

COMMONLY CALLED

THE HOLY EUCHARIST
Renewed Ancient Text

A hymn, psalm, or anthem may be sung.

THE ACCLAMATION

The People standing, the Celebrant says this or a seasonal greeting (pages 145-146)

Blessed be God: the Father, the Son, and the Holy Spirit.

People **And blessed be his kingdom, now and for ever. Amen.**

In the season of Lent

Celebrant Bless the Lord who forgives all our sins.
People **His mercy endures for ever.**

From Easter Day until the Eve of Pentecost

Celebrant Alleluia! Christ is risen!
People **The Lord is risen indeed! Alleluia!**

THE COLLECT FOR PURITY

The Celebrant prays (and the People may be invited to join)

Almighty God, to you all hearts are open, all desires known, and from you no secrets are hid: Cleanse the thoughts of our hearts by the inspiration of your Holy Spirit, that we may perfectly love you, and worthily magnify your holy Name; through Christ our Lord. **Amen.**

THE SUMMARY OF THE LAW

Then follows the Summary of the Law, or The Decalogue (page 100).

Hear what our Lord Jesus Christ says:
You shall love the Lord your God with all your heart and with all your soul and with all your mind. This is the first and great commandment. And the second is like it: You shall love your neighbor as yourself. On these two commandments depend all the Law and the Prophets.
MATTHEW 22:37-40[T]

THE KYRIE

The Celebrant and people pray

Lord, have mercy upon us.	Lord, have mercy.	Kyrie eleison.
Christ, have mercy upon us. *or*	**Christ, have mercy.** *or*	Christe eleison.
Lord, have mercy upon us.	Lord, have mercy.	Kyrie eleison.

or this

THE TRISAGION

Holy God,
Holy and Mighty,
Holy Immortal One,
Have mercy upon us.

The Gloria or some other song of praise may be sung or said, all standing. It is appropriate to omit the song of praise during penitential seasons and days appointed for fasting.

Glory to God in the highest,
    and peace to his people on earth.
Lord God, heavenly King,
almighty God and Father,
    we worship you, we give you thanks,
    we praise you for your glory.
Lord Jesus Christ, only Son of the Father,
Lord God, Lamb of God,
you take away the sin of the world:
    have mercy on us;
you are seated at the right hand of the Father:
    receive our prayer.
For you alone are the Holy One,
you alone are the Lord,
you alone are the Most High,
    Jesus Christ,
    with the Holy Spirit,
    in the glory of God the Father. Amen.

THE COLLECT OF THE DAY

The Celebrant says to the People

	The Lord be with you.
People	**And with your spirit.**
Celebrant	Let us pray.

The Celebrant prays the Collect.

People	**Amen.**

One or more Lessons, as appointed, are read, the Reader first saying

A Reading from _____.

A citation giving chapter and verse may be added.

After each Lesson the Reader may say

The Word of the Lord.
People **Thanks be to God.**

Or the Reader may say Here ends the Reading.

Silence may follow.

A psalm, hymn, or anthem may follow each reading.

All standing, the Deacon or Priest reads the Gospel, first saying

The Holy Gospel of our Lord Jesus Christ according to _____.

People **Glory to you, Lord Christ.**

After the Gospel, the Reader says

The Gospel of the Lord.
People **Praise to you, Lord Christ.**

THE SERMON

THE NICENE CREED

On Sundays, other Major Feast Days, and other times as appointed, all stand to recite the Nicene Creed, the Celebrant first saying

Let us confess our faith in the words of the Nicene Creed:

Celebrant and People

We believe in one God,
   the Father, the Almighty,
   maker of heaven and earth,
   of all that is, visible and invisible.

We believe in one Lord, Jesus Christ,
   the only-begotten Son of God,
   eternally begotten of the Father,
   God from God, Light from Light,
   true God from true God,
   begotten, not made,
   of one Being with the Father;
   through him all things were made.
   For us and for our salvation he came down from heaven,
   was incarnate from the Holy Spirit and the Virgin Mary,
   and was made man.
   For our sake he was crucified under Pontius Pilate;
   he suffered death and was buried.
   On the third day he rose again in accordance with the Scriptures;
   he ascended into heaven
   and is seated at the right hand of the Father.
   He will come again in glory to judge the living and the dead,
   and his kingdom will have no end.

We believe in the Holy Spirit, the Lord, the giver of life,
   who proceeds from the Father [and the Son],†
   who with the Father and the Son is worshiped and glorified,
   who has spoken through the prophets.
   We believe in one holy catholic and apostolic Church.
   We acknowledge one Baptism for the forgiveness of sins.
   We look for the resurrection of the dead,
   and the life of the world to come. Amen.

---

† *The phrase "and the Son" (Latin* filioque*) is not in the original Greek text. See the resolution of the College of Bishops concerning the* filioque *in Documentary Foundations (page 768).*

*The Deacon or other person appointed says these prayers, or the Prayers of the
People in the Anglican Standard Text. The reader pauses after each bidding, and
the people may add petitions, either silently or aloud.*

Let us pray for the Church and for the world, saying,
"hear our prayer."

For the peace of the whole world, and for the well-being and
unity of the people of God.
    Reader   Lord, in your mercy:
    People   **Hear our prayer.**

For *N.*, our Archbishop, and *N.*, our Bishop, and for all the
clergy and people of our Diocese and Congregation.
    Reader   Lord, in your mercy:
    People   **Hear our prayer.**

For all those who proclaim the Gospel at home and abroad; and
for all who teach and disciple others.
    Reader   Lord, in your mercy:
    People   **Hear our prayer.**

For our brothers and sisters in Christ who are persecuted for
their faith.
    Reader   Lord, in your mercy:
    People   **Hear our prayer.**

For our nation, for those in authority, and for all in public
service [especially _____].
    Reader   Lord, in your mercy:
    People   **Hear our prayer.**

For all those who are in trouble, sorrow, need, sickness, or any other adversity [especially _____].

> Reader   Lord, in your mercy:
> People   **Hear our prayer.**

For all those who have departed this life in the certain hope of the resurrection, [especially _____,] in thanksgiving let us pray.

> Reader   Lord, in your mercy:
> People   **Hear our prayer.**

Additional petitions may be added. Thanksgivings may also be invited.

The Celebrant concludes with this or some other appropriate Collect.

Heavenly Father, grant these our prayers for the sake of Jesus Christ, our only Mediator and Advocate, who lives and reigns with you in the unity of the Holy Spirit, one God, now and for ever. **Amen.**

The Celebrant may then say the Exhortation.

THE CONFESSION AND ABSOLUTION OF SIN

The Deacon or other person appointed says the following

Let us humbly confess our sins to Almighty God.

Silence

Most merciful God,
 we confess that we have sinned against you
 in thought, word, and deed,
 by what we have done, and by what we have left undone.
We have not loved you with our whole heart;
 we have not loved our neighbors as ourselves.
We are truly sorry and we humbly repent.
For the sake of your Son Jesus Christ,
 have mercy on us and forgive us;
 that we may delight in your will, and walk in your ways,
 to the glory of your Name. Amen.

The Bishop or Priest stands and says

Almighty God, our heavenly Father, who in his great mercy has promised forgiveness of sins to all those who sincerely repent and with true faith turn to him, have mercy upon you, pardon and deliver you from all your sins, confirm and strengthen you in all goodness, and bring you to everlasting life; through Jesus Christ our Lord. **Amen.**

THE COMFORTABLE WORDS

The Celebrant may then say one or more of the following sentences, first saying

Hear the Word of God to all who truly turn to him.

Come to me, all who labor and are heavy laden, and I will give you rest.   MATTHEW 11:28

God so loved the world, that he gave his only-begotten Son, that whoever believes in him should not perish but have eternal life.   JOHN 3:16[T]

The saying is trustworthy and deserving of full acceptance, that Christ Jesus came into the world to save sinners.

I TIMOTHY 1:15

If anyone sins, we have an advocate with the Father, Jesus Christ the righteous. He is the propitiation for our sins, and not for ours only, but also for the sins of the whole world. I JOHN 2:1-2[T]

THE PEACE

Celebrant The Peace of the Lord be always with you.
  People **And with your spirit.**

Then the Ministers and People may greet one another in the Name of the Lord.

THE OFFERTORY

The Celebrant may begin the Offertory with one of the provided sentences of Scripture.

During the Offertory a hymn, psalm, or anthem may be sung. The Deacon or Priest prepares the Holy Table for the celebration. Representatives of the Congregation may bring the People's offerings of bread and wine, and money or other gifts, to the Deacon or Priest.

The People stand while the offerings are presented. The following may be said.

Celebrant Yours, O LORD, is the greatness, and the power, and the glory, and the victory, and the majesty: for everything in heaven and on earth is yours; yours is the kingdom, O LORD, and you are exalted as Head above all. All things come from you, O LORD,
  People **And of your own have we given you.**

I CHRONICLES 29:11, 14[T]

THE SURSUM CORDA

The People remain standing. The Celebrant faces them and sings or says

The Lord be with you.
People **And with your spirit.**
Celebrant Lift up your hearts.
People **We lift them up to the Lord.**
Celebrant Let us give thanks to the Lord our God.
People **It is right to give him thanks and praise.**

The Celebrant continues

It is right, our duty and our joy, always and everywhere to give thanks to you, Father Almighty, Creator of heaven and earth.

Here a Proper Preface (pages 152-158) is normally sung or said

Therefore we praise you, joining our voices with Angels and Archangels and with all the company of heaven, who for ever sing this hymn to proclaim the glory of your Name:

THE SANCTUS

Celebrant and People

Holy, Holy, Holy, Lord God of power and might, heaven and
   earth are full of your glory.
   Hosanna in the highest.
Blessed is he who comes in the Name of the Lord.
   Hosanna in the highest.

THE PRAYER OF CONSECRATION

The People stand or kneel. The Celebrant continues

Holy and gracious Father: In your infinite love you made us for yourself; and when we had sinned against you and become subject to evil and death, you, in your mercy, sent your only Son Jesus Christ into the world for our salvation. By the Holy Spirit and the Virgin Mary he became flesh and dwelt among us. In obedience to your will, he stretched out his arms upon the Cross and offered himself once for all, that by his suffering and death we might be saved. By his resurrection he broke the bonds of death, trampling Hell and Satan under his feet. As our great high priest, he ascended to your right hand in glory, that we might come with confidence before the throne of grace.

At the following words concerning the bread, the Celebrant is to hold it, or lay a hand upon it, and here* may break the bread; and at the words concerning the cup, to hold or place a hand upon the cup and any other vessel containing the wine to be consecrated.

On the night that he was betrayed, our Lord Jesus Christ took bread; and when he had given thanks, he broke it,* and gave it to his disciples, saying, "Take, eat; this is my Body, which is given for you: Do this in remembrance of me."

Likewise, after supper, Jesus took the cup, and when he had given thanks, he gave it to them, saying, "Drink this, all of you; for this is my Blood of the New Covenant, which is shed for you, and for many, for the forgiveness of sins: Whenever you drink it, do this in remembrance of me."

Therefore we proclaim the mystery of faith:

Celebrant and People

> **Christ has died.**
> **Christ is risen.**
> **Christ will come again.**

We celebrate the memorial of our redemption, O Father, in this sacrifice of praise and thanksgiving, and we offer you these gifts.

Sanctify them by your Word and Holy Spirit to be for your people the Body and Blood of your Son Jesus Christ. Sanctify us also, that we may worthily receive this holy Sacrament, and be made one body with him, that he may dwell in us and we in him. In the fullness of time, put all things in subjection under your Christ, and bring us with all your saints into the joy of your heavenly kingdom, where we shall see our Lord face to face.

All this we ask through your Son Jesus Christ: By him, and with him, and in him, in the unity of the Holy Spirit, all honor and glory is yours, Almighty Father, now and for ever. **Amen.**

THE LORD'S PRAYER

The Celebrant then says

And now as our Savior Christ has taught us, we are bold to pray:

Celebrant and People together pray

Our Father, who art in heaven,
    hallowed be thy Name,
    thy kingdom come,
    thy will be done,
    on earth as it is in heaven.
Give us this day our daily bread.
And forgive us our trespasses,
    as we forgive those
    who trespass against us.
And lead us not into temptation,
    but deliver us from evil.
For thine is the kingdom,
    and the power, and the glory,
    for ever and ever. Amen.
	Our Father in heaven,
	    hallowed be your Name,
	    your kingdom come,
	    your will be done,
	    on earth as it is in heaven.
	Give us today our daily bread.
	And forgive us our sins
	    as we forgive those
	    who sin against us.
	Save us from the time of trial,
	    and deliver us from evil.
	For the kingdom, the power,
	    and the glory are yours,
	    now and for ever. Amen.

If the consecrated Bread was not broken earlier, the Celebrant breaks it now.
A period of silence is kept.

Then may be sung or said

Celebrant	[Alleluia.] Christ our Passover is sacrificed for us.
People	**Therefore let us keep the feast. [Alleluia.]**

or this

Celebrant	[Alleluia.] Christ our Passover Lamb has been sacrificed, once for all upon the Cross.
People	**Therefore let us keep the feast. [Alleluia.]**

In Lent, Alleluia is omitted, and may be omitted at other times except during Easter Season.

THE PRAYER OF HUMBLE ACCESS

Celebrant and People together may say

We do not presume to come to this your table, O merciful Lord,
    trusting in our own righteousness,
      but in your abundant and great mercies.
We are not worthy so much as to gather up
    the crumbs under your table;
      but you are the same Lord
    whose character is always to have mercy.
Grant us, therefore, gracious Lord,
    so to eat the flesh of your dear Son Jesus Christ,
    and to drink his blood,
      that our sinful bodies may be made clean by his body,
      and our souls washed through his most precious blood,
      and that we may evermore dwell in him, and he in us. Amen.

THE AGNUS DEI

The following or some other suitable anthem may be sung or said here

Lamb of God, you take away the sin of the world;
   have mercy on us.
Lamb of God, you take away the sin of the world;
   have mercy on us.
Lamb of God, you take away the sin of the world;
   grant us your peace.

THE MINISTRATION OF COMMUNION

Facing the People, the Celebrant may say the following invitation

The gifts of God for the people of God. [Take them in remembrance that Christ died for you and feed on him in your hearts by faith, with thanksgiving.]

or this

Behold the Lamb of God, behold him who takes away the sins of the world. Blessed are those who are invited to the marriage supper of the Lamb.   JOHN 1:29[T], REVELATION 19:9

The Ministers receive the Sacrament in both kinds, and then immediately deliver it to the People.

The Bread and Cup are given to the communicants with these words

The Body of Christ, the bread of heaven.

The Blood of Christ, the cup of salvation.

During the ministration of Communion, hymns, psalms, or anthems may be sung.

The Celebrant may offer a sentence of Scripture at the conclusion of the Communion.

After Communion, the Celebrant says

Let us pray.

Celebrant and People together say the following, or the Post Communion Prayer in the Anglican Standard Text

Heavenly Father,
We thank you for feeding us with the spiritual food
    of the most precious Body and Blood
    of your Son our Savior Jesus Christ;
    and for assuring us in these holy mysteries
    that we are living members of the body of your Son,
    and heirs of your eternal kingdom.
And now, Father, send us out to do the work you have
    given us to do,
    to love and serve you as faithful witnesses of Christ our Lord.
To him, to you, and to the Holy Spirit,
    be honor and glory, now and for ever. Amen.

THE BLESSING

The Bishop when present, or the Priest, gives this or an alternate blessing

The peace of God, which passes all understanding, keep your hearts and minds in the knowledge and love of God, and of his Son Jesus Christ our Lord; and the blessing of God Almighty, the Father, the Son, and the Holy Spirit, be among you, and remain with you always. **Amen.**

A hymn, psalm, or anthem may be sung after the Blessing (or following the Dismissal).

The Deacon, or the Priest, may dismiss the People with these words

> Let us go forth in the Name of Christ.
> *People* **Thanks be to God.**

or this

> *Deacon* Go in peace to love and serve the Lord.
> *People* **Thanks be to God.**

or this

> *Deacon* Let us go forth into the world, rejoicing in the power
> of the Holy Spirit.
> *People* **Thanks be to God.**

or this

> *Deacon* Let us bless the Lord.
> *People* **Thanks be to God.**

From the Easter Vigil through the Day of Pentecost, "Alleluia, alleluia" is added to any of the dismissals. It may be added at other times, except during Lent and on other penitential occasions.

The People respond

> **Thanks be to God. Alleluia, alleluia.**

OCCASIONAL
PRAYERS

CONTENTS

THE CHURCH

CREATION

THE NATION

Specific to Canada

34. FOR THE SOVEREIGN
35. FOR THE ROYAL FAMILY
36. FOR THE PRIME MINISTER OF CANADA,
    LIEUTENANT GOVERNORS, AND PREMIERS OF THE PROVINCES

Specific to the United States or Mexico

37. FOR THE PRESIDENT AND ALL IN CIVIL AUTHORITY
38. FOR CONGRESS OR A STATE LEGISLATURE
39. FOR OUR NATION

SOCIETY

40. FOR ALL SORTS AND CONDITIONS OF MEN
41. FOR CITIES, TOWNS, AND OTHER COMMUNITIES
42. FOR THE HUMAN FAMILY
43. FOR SOCIAL JUSTICE
44. IN TIMES OF SOCIAL CONFLICT OR DISTRESS
45. FOR THOSE WHO SERVE OTHERS
46. FOR COMMERCE AND INDUSTRY
47. FOR THE UNEMPLOYED
48. FOR AGRICULTURE AND FARMING
49. FOR SCHOOLS, COLLEGES, AND UNIVERSITIES
50. FOR THE MEDICAL PROFESSIONS
51. FOR THOSE WHO INFORM PUBLIC OPINION

THOSE IN NEED

52. FOR THOSE WE LOVE
53. FOR THOSE WHO TRAVEL
54. FOR THE ABSENT
55. FOR THOSE WHO LIVE ALONE
56. FOR THE ELDERLY
57. FOR THOSE WITH CHRONIC DISEASE
58. FOR A PERSON IN TROUBLE OR BEREAVEMENT
59. FOR THE DISCOURAGED AND DOWNCAST
60. FOR PRISONERS
61. FOR THE RECOVERY OF A SICK PERSON
62. FOR THOSE AFFLICTED WITH MENTAL SUFFERING
63. FOR THOSE IN BONDAGE TO ADDICTION
64. FOR THE UNREPENTANT

FAMILY AND PERSONAL LIFE

Throughout The Day

PERSONAL DEVOTION

AT TIMES OF PRAYER AND WORSHIP

DEATH, THE DEPARTED, AND
THE COMMUNION OF SAINTS

THANKSGIVINGS

While most of the prayers included on this list have been rendered in a contemporary idiom, some prayers, because of broad familiarity or difficulty in contemporizing, remain in traditional language.

THE CHURCH

1. FOR THE UNIVERSAL CHURCH

O God of unchangeable power and eternal light: Look favorably on your whole Church, that wonderful and sacred mystery; by the effectual working of your providence, carry out in tranquility the plan of salvation; let the whole world see and know that things which were cast down are being raised up, and things which had grown old are being made new, and that all things are being brought to their perfection by him through whom all things were made, your Son Jesus Christ our Lord; who lives and reigns with you, in the unity of the Holy Spirit, one God, for ever and ever. **Amen.**

2. FOR THE UNIVERSAL CHURCH   *William Laud*

Gracious Father, we pray for your holy Catholic Church. Fill it with all truth, in all truth with all peace. Where it is corrupt, purify it; where it is in error, direct it; where in anything it is amiss, reform it. Where it is right, strengthen it; where it is in want, provide for it; where it is divided, reunite it; for the sake of Jesus Christ your Son our Savior. **Amen.**

3. FOR THE UNITY OF THE CHURCH

Lord Jesus Christ, you said to your apostles, "Peace I give to you; my own peace I leave with you": Regard not our sins, but the faith of your Church, and give to us the peace and unity of that heavenly city, where with the Father and the Holy Spirit you live and reign, now and for ever. **Amen.**

4. FOR THE UNITY OF ALL CHRISTIAN PEOPLE

O God the Father of our Lord Jesus Christ, our only Savior, the Prince of Peace: Give us grace to take to heart the grave dangers we are in through our many divisions. Deliver your Church from all enmity and prejudice, and everything that hinders us from godly union. As there is one Body and one Spirit, one hope of our calling, one Lord, one Faith, one Baptism, one God and Father of us all, so make us all to be of one heart and of one mind, united in one holy bond of truth and peace, of faith and love, that with one voice we may give you praise; through Jesus Christ our Lord, who lives and reigns with you and the Holy Spirit, one God in everlasting glory. **Amen.**

5. FOR THE SPIRIT OF PRAYER

O Almighty God, you pour out on all who desire it the spirit of grace and of supplication: Deliver us, when we draw near to you, from coldness of heart and wanderings of mind, that with steadfast thoughts and kindled affections we may worship you in spirit and in truth; through Jesus Christ our Lord. **Amen.**

6. FOR A PROVINCE OR DIOCESE

O God, by your grace you have called us in *this Diocese* to be a good and godly fellowship of faith. Bless our Bishop(s) *N.*, and other clergy, and all our people. Grant that your Word may be truly preached and truly heard, your Sacraments faithfully administered and faithfully received. By your Spirit, fashion our lives according to the example of your Son, and grant that we may show the power of your love to all among whom we live; through Jesus Christ our Lord. **Amen.**

7. FOR A PROVINCIAL OR DIOCESAN CONVENTION OR SYNOD

Almighty and everlasting God, by your Holy Spirit you presided in the council of the blessed Apostles, and you promised, through your Son Jesus Christ, to be with your Church to the end of the world: Be with the council of your Church assembled

[here] in your Name and presence. Save us from all error, ignorance, prejudice, and pride; and of your great mercy direct, sanctify, and govern us in our work, by the mighty power of the Holy Spirit; that the order and discipline of your Church may be maintained, and that the Gospel of Christ may be truly preached, truly received, and truly followed in all places, breaking down the kingdom of sin, Satan, and death; till all your scattered sheep, being gathered into one fold, become partakers of everlasting life; through the merits and death of Jesus Christ our Savior. **Amen.**

8. FOR A PROVINCIAL OR DIOCESAN CONVENTION OR SYNOD

Gracious and everliving Father, you have given the Holy Spirit to abide with us for ever: Bless, we pray, with the Holy Spirit's grace and presence, the Bishop(s), Priests, Deacons, and all the Laity who assemble in your Name; that your Church, being preserved in true faith and godly discipline, may fulfill the will of him who loved her and gave himself for her, your Son Jesus Christ our Savior; who now lives and reigns with you and the same Spirit, one God, now and for ever. **Amen.**

9. FOR VESTRY AND CHURCH MEETINGS

Almighty and everliving God, source of all wisdom and understanding, be present with those who take counsel [in _____] for the renewal and mission of your Church. Teach us in all things to seek first your honor and glory. Guide us to perceive what is right, and grant us both the courage to pursue it and the grace to accomplish it; through Jesus Christ our Lord. **Amen.**

10. FOR THE SELECTION OF A BISHOP OR OTHER MINISTER

Almighty God, giver of every good gift: Look graciously on your Church, and so guide the minds of those who shall choose a *Bishop* for this *Diocese* that we may receive a faithful pastor who will preach the Gospel, care for your people, equip us for ministry, and lead us forth in fulfillment of the Great Commission; through Jesus Christ our Lord. **Amen.**

11. FOR THE LOCAL CONGREGATION

O God the Holy Spirit, Sanctifier of the faithful: Sanctify this *Congregation* by your abiding presence. Bless those who minister in holy things. Enlighten the minds of your people more and more with the light of the everlasting Gospel. Bring erring souls to the knowledge of our Savior Jesus Christ; and those who are walking in the way of life, keep steadfast to the end. Give patience to the sick and afflicted, and renew them in body and soul. Guard those who are strong and prosperous from forgetting you. Increase in us your many gifts of grace, and make us all fruitful in good works. This we ask, O blessed Spirit, whom with the Father and the Son we worship and glorify, one God, world without end. **Amen.**

12. FOR THE LOCAL CONGREGATION

Almighty and everlasting God, you govern all things in heaven and on earth: Mercifully hear our prayers, and grant that in this *Congregation* the pure Word of God may be preached and the Sacraments duly administered. Strengthen and confirm the faithful; protect and guide the children; visit and relieve the sick; turn and soften the wicked; arouse the careless; recover the fallen; restore the penitent; remove all hindrances to the advancement of your truth; and bring us all to be of one heart and mind within your holy Church, to the honor and glory of your Name; through Jesus Christ our Lord. **Amen.**

13. FOR VOCATIONS TO ORDAINED MINISTRY

Lord Jesus, you are the Good Shepherd who cares for his flock:
We ask you to bestow upon your Church the gifts of the Holy
Spirit in abundance, and to raise up from among us faithful
and able persons called to the ministries of Deacon, Priest, and
Bishop. Inspire them to spend and be spent for the sake of the
Gospel, and make them holy and loving servants and shepherds
of the flock for whom you shed your most precious blood. Grant
this for the sake of your love. **Amen.**

See also the Ember Day Collects on page 634

14. FOR CHURCH MUSICIANS AND ARTISTS

O God, whom saints and angels delight to worship in heaven:
Be ever present with your servants on earth who seek through
art and music to perfect the praises of your people. Grant them
even now true glimpses of your beauty, and make them worthy
at length to behold it unveiled for evermore; through Jesus
Christ our Lord. **Amen.**

15. FOR MONASTIC ORDERS AND VOCATIONS

O Lord Jesus Christ, you became poor for our sake that we
might be made rich through your poverty: Guide and sanctify,
we pray, those whom you call to follow you in poverty, chastity,
and obedience; that by their prayer and service they may enrich
your Church, and by their life and worship may glorify your
Name; for you live and reign with the Father and the Holy
Spirit, one God, now and for ever. **Amen.**

16. FOR THE MISSION OF THE CHURCH

O God, you have made of one blood all the peoples of the earth,
and sent your blessed Son to preach peace to those who are far

off and to those who are near: Grant that people everywhere may seek after you and find you; bring the nations into your fold; pour out your Spirit upon all flesh; and hasten the coming of your kingdom; through Jesus Christ our Lord. **Amen.**

17. FOR THE MISSION OF THE CHURCH

O God, our heavenly Father, you manifested your love by sending your only-begotten Son into the world, that all might live through him: Pour out your Spirit on your Church, that we may fulfill his command to preach the Gospel to all people. Send forth laborers into your harvest; defend them in all dangers and temptations; and hasten the time when the fullness of the Gentiles shall be gathered in, and faithful Israel shall be saved; through your Son Jesus Christ our Lord. **Amen.**

See also the Prayers for Mission in Morning and Evening Prayer on pages 24, 25 & 51

18. FOR MISSIONARY SOCIETIES

Lord Jesus, you commanded us to make disciples of all nations: Bless all those who work together for the spread of the Gospel [especially _____]; make them faithful and true witnesses to proclaim your glorious Name. Send down the grace of the Holy Spirit upon all your people, that we may give cheerfully of our substance for the evangelization of the world, and that the light of your truth may shine brightly in every place. Hear us, O merciful Savior, who with the Father and the Holy Spirit live and reign, one God, world without end. **Amen.**

19. FOR ALL MISSIONARIES

O God, you desire that all people be saved and come to
knowledge of the truth: Prosper all those who live, preach,
and teach the Gospel at home and in distant lands [especially
_____]; protect them in all perils, support them in
their loneliness, sustain them in the hour of trial; give them
your abundant grace to bear faithful witness; and endue
them with burning zeal and love, that they may turn many to
righteousness; through Jesus Christ our Lord. **Amen.**

20. FOR A SPIRIT OF EVANGELISM

Almighty God our Savior, you desire that none should perish,
and you have taught us through your Son that there is great joy
in heaven over every sinner who repents: Grant that our hearts
may ache for a lost and broken world. May your Holy Spirit
work through our words, deeds, and prayers, that the lost may
be found and the dead made alive, and that all your redeemed
may rejoice around your throne; through Jesus Christ our Lord.
Amen.

CREATION

21. FOR JOY IN GOD'S CREATION

O heavenly Father, you have filled the world with beauty: Open
our eyes to behold your gracious hand in all your works; that,
rejoicing in your whole creation, we may learn to serve you with
gladness; for the sake of him through whom all things were
made, your Son Jesus Christ our Lord. **Amen.**

22. FOR STEWARDSHIP OF CREATION

O merciful Creator, your loving hand is open wide to satisfy the
needs of every living creature: Make us always thankful for your
loving providence, and give us grace to honor you with all that

you have entrusted to us; that we, remembering the account we must one day give, may be faithful stewards of your good gifts; through Jesus Christ our Lord, who with you and the Holy Spirit lives and reigns, one God, for ever and ever. **Amen.**

23. FOR THE HARVEST OF LANDS AND WATERS

O gracious Father, you open your hand and fill all living things with plenteousness: Bless the lands and waters, and multiply the harvests of the world; send forth your breath, and renew the face of the earth; show your loving-kindness, that our land may yield its increase; and save us from selfish use of what you provide, that the poor and needy may give thanks to your Name; through Jesus Christ our Lord. **Amen.**

See also Prayer 48 and the Rogation Day Collects on page 635

24. FOR RAIN

O God, our heavenly Father, by your Son Jesus Christ you have promised to those who seek your kingdom and its righteousness all things necessary to sustain their life: Send us, we pray, in this time of need, such moderate rain and showers, that we may receive the fruits of the earth, to our comfort and to your honor; through Jesus Christ our Lord. **Amen.**

25. IN TIME OF SCARCITY AND FAMINE

O God, our heavenly Father, whose blessed Son has taught us to seek our daily bread from you: Behold the affliction of your people, and send *us* swift aid in *our* time of need. Increase the fruits of the earth by your heavenly benediction; and grant that we, receiving your gifts with thankful hearts, may use them to your glory, for the relief of those in need, and for our own health; through Jesus Christ our Lord. **Amen.**

26. IN TIMES OF NATURAL DISASTER

Almighty God, by your Word you laid the foundations of the earth, set the bounds of the sea, and still the wind and waves. Surround us with your grace and peace, and preserve us through this *storm* [*or* _____]. By your Spirit, lift up those who have fallen, strengthen those who work to rescue or rebuild, and fill us with the hope of your new creation; through Jesus Christ our Lord. **Amen.**

THE NATION

27. FOR THE PEACE OF THE WORLD

Eternal God, in whose perfect kingdom no sword is drawn but the sword of righteousness, no strength known but the strength of love: So mightily spread abroad your Spirit, that all peoples may be gathered under the banner of the Prince of Peace; to whom be dominion and glory, now and for ever. **Amen.**

28. FOR THE PEACE OF THE WORLD

Almighty God, from whom all thoughts of truth and peace proceed: Kindle, we pray, in the hearts of all people the true love of peace, and guide with your pure and peaceable wisdom those who take counsel for the nations of the earth; that in tranquility your kingdom may go forward, till the earth is filled with the knowledge of your love; through Jesus Christ our Lord. **Amen.**

29. FOR COURTS OF JUSTICE

Almighty God, you sit on your throne giving righteous judgment: We humbly ask you to bless all courts of justice and all magistrates in this land; give them a spirit of wisdom and understanding, that fearing no power but yours alone, they may discern the truth and impartially administer the law; through him who shall come to be our Judge, your Son our Savior Jesus Christ. **Amen.**

30. FOR CIVIL AUTHORITIES

Almighty God, our heavenly Father, send down on those who hold public office [especially _____] the spirit of wisdom, charity, and justice; that with steadfast purpose they may faithfully serve in their offices to promote the well-being of all people; through Jesus Christ our Lord. **Amen.**

31. FOR AN ELECTION

Almighty God, to whom we must account for all our powers and privileges: Guide and direct, we humbly pray, the minds of all those who are called to elect fit persons to serve [in _____]. Grant that in the exercise of *our* choice *we* may promote your glory, and the welfare of this *nation*. This we ask for the sake of our Lord and Savior Jesus Christ. **Amen.**

32. FOR THOSE IN THE ARMED FORCES

Almighty God, we commend to your gracious care and keeping all the men and women of our armed forces at home and abroad. Defend them day by day with your heavenly grace; strengthen them in their trials and temptations; give them courage to face the perils which beset them; and grant them a sense of your abiding presence wherever they may be; through Jesus Christ our Lord. **Amen.**

33. FOR OUR ENEMIES

O God, the Creator of all, whose Son commanded us to love our enemies: Lead them and us from prejudice to truth; deliver them and us from hatred, cruelty, and revenge; and in your good time enable us all to stand reconciled before you in Jesus Christ; in whose Name we pray. **Amen.**

34. FOR THE SOVEREIGN

Almighty and everlasting God, we are taught by your holy Word that the hearts of kings are in your rule, and that you direct them according to your wisdom: We humbly ask you so to govern the heart of *N.* your servant, our *Queen* and Governor, that in all *her* thoughts, words, and deeds, *she* may ever seek your honour and glory, and act to preserve your people committed to *her* charge in prosperity, peace, and godliness; Grant this, O merciful Father, for the sake of your dear Son Jesus Christ our Lord. **Amen.**

35. FOR THE ROYAL FAMILY

Almighty God, the fountain of all goodness, we humbly ask you to bless our most gracious Sovereign, *Queen N.*, [*here may be named other members of the Royal Family*] and all the Royal Family: Endue them with your Holy Spirit; enrich them with your heavenly grace; prosper them with all happiness; and bring them to your everlasting kingdom; through Jesus Christ our Lord. **Amen.**

36. FOR THE PRIME MINISTER OF CANADA, LIEUTENANT GOVERNORS, AND THE PREMIERS OF THE PROVINCES

Lord of all power and mercy, we ask you to assist with your favour the Governor General and Prime Minister, and the Lieutenant Governors and Premiers of the Provinces. Cause them to walk before you in truth and righteousness, and to fulfill their office to your glory and the public good; through Jesus Christ our Lord. **Amen.**

37. FOR THE PRESIDENT AND ALL IN CIVIL AUTHORITY

O Lord our Governor, whose glory fills all the world: We commend this Nation to your merciful care, that we may be guided by your providence, and dwell secure in your peace. Grant to the President of this Nation, the Governor of this State [*or* Commonwealth], and to all in authority, wisdom and strength to know and to do your will. Fill them with the love of truth and righteousness, and make them continually mindful of their calling to serve this people in reverent obedience to you; through Jesus Christ our Lord, who lives and reigns with you and the Holy Spirit, one God, world without end. **Amen.**

38. FOR CONGRESS OR A STATE LEGISLATURE

O God, the fountain of wisdom, whose will is good and gracious, and whose law is truth: So guide and bless our Senators and Representatives assembled in Congress [*or* the Legislature of this State, Commonwealth, etc.], that they may enact laws pleasing in your sight, to the glory of your Name and the welfare of this people; through Jesus Christ our Lord. **Amen.**

39. FOR OUR NATION

Almighty God, who hast given us this good land for our heritage: We humbly beseech thee that we may always prove ourselves a people mindful of thy favor and glad to do thy will. Bless our land with honorable industry, sound learning, and pure conduct. Save us from violence, discord, and confusion; from pride and arrogance, and from every evil way. Defend our liberties, and fashion into one united people the multitudes brought hither out of many kindreds and tongues. Endue with

the spirit of wisdom those to whom, in thy Name, we entrust
the authority of government, that there may be justice and peace
at home, and that, through obedience to thy law, we may show
forth thy praise among the nations of the earth. In the time of
prosperity, fill our hearts with thankfulness, and in the day of
trouble, suffer not our trust in thee to fail; all of which we ask
through Jesus Christ our Lord. **Amen.**

SOCIETY

40. FOR ALL SORTS AND CONDITIONS OF MEN

O God, the creator and preserver of all mankind, we humbly
beseech thee for all sorts and conditions of men; that thou
wouldest be pleased to make thy ways known unto them, thy
saving health unto all nations. More especially we pray for thy
holy Church universal, that it may be so guided and governed
by thy good Spirit, that all who profess and call themselves
Christians may be led into the way of truth, and hold the faith
in unity of spirit, in the bond of peace, and in righteousness of
life. Finally, we commend to thy fatherly goodness all those who
are in any ways afflicted or distressed, in mind, body, or estate,
[especially those for whom our prayers are desired]; that it
may please thee to comfort and relieve them according to their
several necessities, giving them patience under their sufferings,
and a happy issue out of all their afflictions. And this we beg for
Jesus Christ's sake. **Amen.**

41. FOR CITIES, TOWNS, AND OTHER COMMUNITIES

Heavenly Father, you sent your Son among us to proclaim
the kingdom of God in cities, towns, villages, and lonely
places. Behold and visit, we pray, the community of _____.
Renew the bonds of charity that uphold our civic life. Send
us honest and able leaders. Deliver us from poverty, prejudice,

and oppression, that peace may prevail with righteousness, and justice with mercy. And at the last, bring us to your Holy City, the new Jerusalem, where we shall know perfect unity and peace; through Jesus Christ our Lord. **Amen.**

42. FOR THE HUMAN FAMILY

O God, you made us in your own image, and you have redeemed us through your Son Jesus Christ: Look with compassion on the whole human family; take away the arrogance and hatred which infect our hearts; break down the walls that separate us; unite us in bonds of love; and work through our struggle and confusion to accomplish your purposes on earth; that, in your good time, all nations and races may serve you in harmony around your heavenly throne; through Jesus Christ our Lord. **Amen.**

43. FOR SOCIAL JUSTICE

Almighty God, you created us in your own image: Grant us grace to contend fearlessly against evil and to make no peace with oppression; and help us to use our freedom rightly in the establishment of justice in our communities and among the nations, to the glory of your holy Name; through Jesus Christ our Lord, who lives and reigns with you and the Holy Spirit, one God, now and for ever. **Amen.**

44. IN TIMES OF SOCIAL CONFLICT OR DISTRESS

Increase, O God, the spirit of neighborliness among us, that in peril we may uphold one another, in suffering tend to one another, and in homelessness, loneliness, or exile befriend one another. Grant us brave and enduring hearts that we may strengthen one another, until the disciplines and testing of these days are ended, and you again give peace in our time; through Jesus Christ our Lord. **Amen.**

45. FOR THOSE WHO SERVE OTHERS

O Lord our heavenly Father, whose blessed Son came not to
be served, but to serve: We ask you to bless all who, following
in his steps, give themselves to the service of others [especially
_____]; endue them with wisdom, patience, and courage,
that they may strengthen the weak and raise up those who fall,
and, being inspired by your love, may worthily minister to the
suffering, the friendless, and the needy; for the sake of him who
laid down his life for us, your Son our Savior Jesus Christ. **Amen.**

46. FOR COMMERCE AND INDUSTRY

O Lord Jesus Christ, in your earthly life you shared our toil and
hallowed our labor: Guide those who maintain the commerce
and industries of this land, and give to all who labor pride in
their work, a just reward, and joy both in supplying need and in
serving you; who with the Father and the Holy Spirit live and
reign, one God, world without end. **Amen.**

47. FOR THE UNEMPLOYED

Heavenly Father, we remember before you those who suffer
want and anxiety from lack of work. Guide the people of this
land so to use our public and private wealth that all may find
suitable and fulfilling employment, and receive a just reward for
their labor; through Jesus Christ our Lord. **Amen.**

48. FOR AGRICULTURE AND FARMING

Almighty God, we thank you for making the earth fruitful, so
that it may produce what is needed to sustain our life: Bless
those who work in the fields; give us seasonable weather; and
grant that we may all share the fruits of the earth, rejoicing in
your goodness; through Jesus Christ our Lord. **Amen.**

See also Prayer 23 and the Rogation Day Collects on page 635

49. FOR SCHOOLS, COLLEGES, AND UNIVERSITIES

Almighty God, by your gift alone we come to wisdom and true understanding: Look with favor, we pray, on our universities, colleges, and schools, [especially _____,] that knowledge may be increased among us, and wholesome learning flourish and abound. Bless those who teach and those who learn; and grant that in humility of heart they may ever look to you, the fountain of all wisdom; through Jesus Christ our Lord. **Amen.**

50. FOR THE MEDICAL PROFESSIONS

Almighty God, whose blessed Son Jesus Christ went about doing good, and healing all manner of sickness and disease among the people: Continue in our *hospitals* his gracious work among us [especially in _____]; console and heal the sick; grant to the physicians, nurses, and assisting staff wisdom and skill, diligence and patience; prosper their work, O Lord, and send down your blessing upon all who serve the suffering; through Jesus Christ our Lord. **Amen.**

51. FOR THOSE WHO INFORM PUBLIC OPINION

Almighty God, your truth endures from age to age: Direct in our time, we pray, those who speak where many listen and write what many read; that they may speak your truth to make the heart of this people wise, its mind discerning, and its will righteous; to the honor of Jesus Christ our Lord. **Amen.**

THOSE IN NEED

52. FOR THOSE WE LOVE

Almighty God, we entrust all who are dear to us [especially
_____] to your never-failing care and love, for this life and the life
to come, knowing that you are doing for *them* better things than
we can desire or pray for; through Jesus Christ our Lord. **Amen.**

See also Additional Prayers in Family Prayer on pages 76–78

53. FOR THOSE WHO TRAVEL

O God, our heavenly Father, whose glory fills the whole
creation, and whose presence we find wherever we go: Preserve
those who travel [especially _____]; surround *them* with your
loving care; protect *them* from every danger; and bring *them* in
safety to their journey's end; through Jesus Christ our Lord.
Amen.

54. FOR THE ABSENT

O God, whose fatherly care reaches to the ends of the earth:
We ask you graciously to behold and bless those we love who
are now absent from us [especially _____]. Defend them from
all dangers of soul and body, and grant that both they and we,
drawing nearer to you, may be bound together by your love, in
the communion of your Holy Spirit and in the fellowship of
your saints; through Jesus Christ our Lord. **Amen.**

55. FOR THOSE WHO LIVE ALONE

Almighty God, whose Son had nowhere to lay his head: Grant
that all those who live alone [especially _____] may not be
lonely in their solitude, but that, following in his steps, they may
find fulfillment in loving you and their neighbors; through Jesus
Christ our Lord. **Amen.**

56. FOR THE ELDERLY

Look with mercy, O God our Father, on all whose increasing years bring them weakness, distress, or isolation [especially _____]. Provide for *them* homes of dignity and peace; give *them* understanding helpers, and the willingness to accept help; and as *their* strength diminishes, increase *their* faith and *their* assurance of your love; through Jesus Christ our Lord. **Amen.**

57. FOR THOSE WITH CHRONIC DISEASE

Heavenly Father, sustainer of our life and source of our hope: Comfort and relieve all who endure long-term illness or persistent handicap [especially _____]. Give your grace to all who minister to *their* needs, that *they* may be strengthened in *their* weakness and have confidence in your loving care; through him who knows our weakness and has shared our sorrows, Jesus Christ our Lord. **Amen.**

58. FOR A PERSON IN TROUBLE OR BEREAVEMENT

O merciful Father, you have taught us in your holy Word that you do not willingly afflict or grieve the children of men: Look with pity on the sorrows of your servant *N.* Remember *him*, O Lord, in mercy; nourish *his* soul with patience; comfort *him* with a sense of your goodness; lift up your countenance upon *him*; and give *him* peace; through Jesus Christ our Lord. **Amen.**

59. FOR THE DISCOURAGED AND DOWNCAST

O God, almighty and merciful, you heal the broken-hearted, and turn the sadness of the sorrowful to joy: Let your fatherly goodness be upon all whom you have made. Remember in pity all those who are this day destitute, homeless, elderly, infirm, or forgotten. Bless the multitude of your poor. Lift up those who are cast down. Mightily befriend innocent sufferers, and sanctify to them the endurance of their wrongs. Cheer with hope all who are discouraged and downcast, and by your heavenly grace preserve from falling those whose poverty tempts them to sin. Though they be troubled on every side, suffer them not to be distressed; though they are perplexed, save them from despair. Grant this, O Lord, for the love of him who for our sakes became poor, your Son our Savior Jesus Christ. **Amen.**

60. FOR PRISONERS

O God, you forgive when we deserve punishment, and in your wrath you remember mercy: We humbly ask you, of your goodness, to comfort all prisoners [and especially those who are condemned to die]. Give them a right understanding of themselves, and of your promises, that trusting wholly in your mercy, they may not place their confidence anywhere but in you. Relieve the distressed; deliver the innocent; bring the guilty to repentance; and as you alone bring light out of darkness, and good out of evil, grant that by the power of your Holy Spirit they may be set free from the chains of sin, and brought to newness of life; through Jesus Christ our Lord. **Amen.**

61. FOR THE RECOVERY OF A SICK PERSON

Almighty and immortal God, giver of life and health: We implore your mercy for your servant *N.*, that by your blessing upon *him* and upon those who minister to *him* with your healing gifts, *he* may be restored to health of body and mind, according to your gracious will, and may give thanks to you in your holy Church; through Jesus Christ our Lord. **Amen.**

See also Additional Prayers in The Rites of Healing on pages 231–235

Almighty God, whose Son took upon himself the afflictions of your people: Regard with your tender compassion those suffering from anxiety, depression, or mental illness [especially _____]; bear *their* sorrows and *their* cares; supply all *their* needs; help *them* to put *their* whole trust and confidence in you; and restore *them* to strength of mind and cheerfulness of spirit; through Jesus Christ our Lord. **Amen.**

63. FOR THOSE IN BONDAGE TO ADDICTION

O blessed Lord, you ministered to all who came to you: Look with compassion upon those who through addiction have lost their health and freedom. Restore to them the assurance of your unfailing mercy; remove from them the fears that beset them; strengthen them in the work of their recovery; and to those who minister to them, give patient understanding and persevering love; through Jesus Christ our Lord. **Amen.**

64. FOR THE UNREPENTANT

Merciful God, you desire not the death of sinners, but rather that they should turn to you and live; and through your only Son you have revealed yourself as the God who pardons iniquity. Have mercy on the unrepentant and those who do not believe [especially _____]. Awaken in *them*, by your Word and Holy Spirit, a deep sense of *their* sinfulness and peril. Take from *them* all ignorance, hardness of heart, and contempt of your Word. Grant *them* to know and feel that there is no other Name under heaven given among men by which they must be saved, but only the Name of the Lord Jesus Christ. And so bring *them* home and number *them* among your children, that *they* may be yours for ever; through Jesus Christ our Lord, who lives and reigns with you and the Holy Spirit, one God, world without end. **Amen.**

65. FOR FAMILIES

Almighty God, our heavenly Father, you set the solitary in
families: We commend to your continual care the homes in
which your people dwell. Put far from them every root of
bitterness, the desire of vainglory, and the pride of life. Fill them
with faith, virtue, knowledge, temperance, patience, and true
godliness. Knit together in constant affection those who, in holy
matrimony, have been made one flesh; turn the hearts of parents
to their children, and the hearts of children to their parents; and
so enkindle fervent charity among us all, that we may evermore
be joined to one another with bonds of loving-kindness;
through Jesus Christ our Lord. **Amen.**

See also Additional Prayers in Family Prayer on pages 76-78

66. FOR THE CARE OF CHILDREN

Almighty God, heavenly Father, you have blessed us with the
joy and care of children: Give us calm strength and patient
wisdom so to train them, that they may love all that is true, and
pure, and lovely, and of good report, following the example of
their Savior Jesus Christ. **Amen.**

67. FOR A BIRTHDAY

O God, our times are in your hand: Look with favor, we pray,
on your servant *N.* as *he* begins another year. Grant that *he* may
grow in wisdom and grace, and strengthen *his* trust in your
goodness all the days of *his* life; through Jesus Christ our Lord.
Amen.

68. FOR A CHILD, OR FOR A BIRTHDAY

Watch over your child *N.*, O Lord, as *his* days increase; bless *him* and guide *him*, and keep *him* unspotted from the world. Strengthen *him* when *he* stands; comfort *him* when discouraged or sorrowful; raise *him* up if *he* falls; and in *his* heart may your peace which passes understanding abide all the days of *his* life; through Jesus Christ our Lord. **Amen.**

69. FOR A MARRIAGE OR ANNIVERSARY

O God, you have so consecrated the covenant of marriage that in it is represented the spiritual unity between Christ and his Church: Send your blessing upon these your servants [as they begin another year], that they may so love, honor, and cherish each other in faithfulness and patience, in wisdom and true godliness, that their home may be a haven of blessing and peace; through Jesus Christ our Lord, who lives and reigns with you and the Holy Spirit, one God, now and for ever. **Amen.**

70. FOR INNER RENEWAL THROUGH THE WORD

Gracious God and most merciful Father, you have granted us the rich and precious jewel of your holy Word: Assist us with your Spirit, that the same Word may be written in our hearts to our everlasting comfort, to reform us, to renew us according to your own image, to build us up and edify us into the perfect dwelling place of your Christ, sanctifying and increasing in us all heavenly virtues; grant this, O heavenly Father, for Jesus Christ's sake. **Amen.**

71. FOR CHRIST TO BE FORMED IN US

Lord Jesus, Master Carpenter of Nazareth, on the Cross through wood and nails you wrought our full salvation: Wield well your tools in this, your workshop, that we who come to you rough-hewn may be fashioned into a truer beauty by your hand; who with the Father and the Holy Spirit live and reign, one God, world without end. **Amen.**

72. FOR KNOWING AND LOVING GOD

O God, the light of the minds that know you, the life of the souls that love you, and the strength of the wills that serve you: Help us so to know you that we may truly love you, and so to love you that we may fully serve you, whom to serve is perfect freedom; through Jesus Christ our Lord. **Amen.**

73. A PRAYER OF SELF-DEDICATION *William Temple*

Almighty and eternal God, so draw our hearts to you, so guide our minds, so fill our imaginations, so control our wills, that we may be wholly yours, utterly dedicated to you; and then use us, we pray, as you will, and always to your glory and the welfare of your people; through our Lord and Savior Jesus Christ. **Amen.**

74. FOR DESIRING GOD *Francis Xavier*

O God, grant that we may desire you, and desiring you seek you, and seeking you find you, and finding you be satisfied in you for ever. **Amen.**

75. FOR HOLY THOUGHT

O God, without whose beauty and goodness our souls are unfed, without whose truth our reason withers: Consecrate our lives to your will, giving us such purity of heart, such depth of faith, and such steadfastness of purpose, that in time we may come to think your own thoughts after you; through Jesus Christ our Savior. **Amen.**

76. FOR GUIDANCE

Go before us, O Lord, in all our doings with your most gracious favor, and further us with your continual help; that in all our works begun, continued, and ended in you, we may glorify your holy Name, and finally, through your mercy, obtain everlasting life; through Jesus Christ our Lord. **Amen.**

77. FOR GUIDANCE

O God, by whom the meek are guided in judgment, and light rises up in darkness for the godly: Grant us, in all our doubts and uncertainties, the grace to ask what you would have us do, that the Spirit of wisdom may save us from all false choices; that in your light we may see light, and in your straight path we may not stumble; through Jesus Christ our Lord. **Amen.**

78. TO PLEASE GOD RATHER THAN MEN   *Thomas à Kempis*

Our God, in whom we trust: Strengthen us not to regard overmuch who is for us or who is against us, but to see to it that we be with you in everything we do. **Amen.**

79. FOR MERCY

Almighty God, you have not dealt with us according to our sins, nor rewarded us according to our iniquities; grant that we, who for our evil deeds deserve to be punished, by the might of your grace may mercifully be relieved; through our Lord and Savior Jesus Christ, who lives and reigns with you and the Holy Spirit, one God, for ever and ever. **Amen.**

80. FOR TRUSTFULNESS IN TIMES OF WORRY AND ANXIETY

Most loving Father, you will us to give thanks for all things, to dread nothing but the loss of you, and to cast all our care on the One who cares for us. Preserve us from faithless fears and worldly anxieties, and grant that no clouds of this mortal life may hide from us the light of that love which is immortal, and which you have manifested unto us in your Son, Jesus Christ our Lord. **Amen.**

81. FOR HELP TO BEAR BEREAVEMENT

Heavenly Father, help us to entrust our loved ones to your care. Though sorrow darkens our lives, help us to look up to you, remembering the cloud of witnesses by which we are surrounded. And grant that we on earth, rejoicing ever in your presence, may share with them the rest and peace which your presence gives; through Jesus Christ our Lord. **Amen.**

82. FOR QUIET CONFIDENCE

O God of peace, who hast taught us that in returning and rest we shall be saved, in quietness and in confidence shall be our strength: By the might of thy Spirit lift us, we pray thee, to thy presence, where we may be still and know that thou art God; through Jesus Christ our Lord. **Amen.**

Throughout the Day

83. IN THE MORNING

Almighty God, you alone gave us the breath of life, and you alone can keep alive in us the holy desires you impart. We beseech you, for your compassion's sake, to sanctify all our thoughts and endeavors, that we may neither begin an action without a pure intention nor continue it without your blessing. And grant that, having the eyes of our mind enlightened to behold things invisible and unseen, we may in heart be inspired by your wisdom, in work be upheld by your strength, and in the end be accepted as your faithful servants; through Jesus Christ our Savior. **Amen.**

See also Morning Prayer (pages 10-26) and Family Prayer (pages 67-68)

84. GRACE AT MEALS

Blessed are you, O Lord God, King of the Universe, for you give us food to sustain our lives and make our hearts glad; through Jesus Christ our Lord. **Amen.**

See also Additional Prayers in Family Prayer on page 78.

85. IN THE EVENING   *John Henry Newman*

O Lord, support us all the day long through this trouble-filled life, until the shadows lengthen, and the evening comes, and the busy world is hushed, and the fever of life is over, and our work is done. Then in your mercy grant us a safe lodging, and a holy rest, and peace at the last. **Amen.**

See also Evening Prayer (pages 41-53), Compline (pages 57-65), and Family Prayer (pages 71-74)

86. FOR SLEEP

Father, in your mercy dispel the darkness of this night, and let your servant sleep in peace, that at the dawn of a new day I may wake with joy in your Name; through Christ our Lord. **Amen.**

87. FOR PARTICIPATION IN THE PEACE OF GOD

In the Tradition of Francis of Assisi

Lord, make me an instrument of your peace: where there is hatred, let me sow love; where there is injury, pardon; where there is discord, union; where there is error, truth; where there is doubt, faith; where there is despair, hope; where there is darkness, light; where there is sadness, joy. O divine Master, grant that I may seek not so much to be consoled as to console, to be understood as to understand, to be loved as to love. For it is in giving that we receive, it is in pardoning that we are pardoned, and it is in dying that we are born to eternal life. **Amen.**

88. FOR DAILY GROWTH

Richard of Chichester

Thanks be to thee, my Lord Jesus Christ, for all the pains and insults thou hast borne for me, and all the benefits thou hast given me. O most merciful Redeemer, Friend, and Brother: Grant that I may see thee more clearly, love thee more dearly, and follow thee more nearly, day by day. **Amen.**

89. FOR SEEKING GOD

Anselm of Canterbury

Teach me to seek you, and as I seek you, show yourself to me; for I cannot seek you unless you show me how, and I will never find you unless you show yourself to me. Let me seek you by desiring you, and desire you by seeking you; let me find you by loving you, and love you in finding you. **Amen.**

90. FOR GRACE TO SEEK GOD IN EVERY WAY *Benedict of Nursia*

Gracious and holy Father, please give me intellect to understand you, reason to discern you, diligence to seek you, wisdom to find you, a spirit to know you, a heart to meditate upon you, ears to hear you, eyes to see you, a tongue to proclaim you, a way of life pleasing to you, patience to wait for you, and perseverance to look for you. Grant me a perfect end, your holy presence, a blessed resurrection, and life everlasting. **Amen.**

91. FOR SUBMISSION TO GOD'S WILL *Joseph Mercier*

O Holy Spirit, beloved of my soul, I adore you. Enlighten me, guide me, strengthen me, console me. Tell me what I should do; give me your orders. I promise to submit myself to all that you desire of me and to accept all that you permit to happen to me. Let me only know your will. **Amen.**

92. FOR SATISFACTION IN CHRIST *Julian of Norwich*

O God, of your goodness, give me yourself, for you are enough for me. I can ask for nothing less that is completely to your honor, and if I do ask anything less, I shall always be in want. Only in you I have all. **Amen.**

93. A COVENANT PRAYER *John Wesley*

I am no longer my own, but thine. Put me to what thou wilt, rank me with whom thou wilt. Put me to doing, put me to suffering. Let me be employed by thee or laid aside for thee, exalted for thee or brought low for thee. Let me be full, let me be empty. Let me have all things, let me have nothing. I freely and heartily yield all things to thy pleasure and disposal. And now, O glorious and blessed God, Father, Son, and Holy Spirit, thou art mine, and I am thine. So be it. And the covenant which I have made on earth, let it be ratified in heaven. **Amen.**

94. FOR A VIRTUOUS HEART *Thomas Aquinas*

Give me, O Lord, a steadfast heart, which no unworthy thought can drag down; an unconquered heart, which no tribulation can wear out; an upright heart, which no unworthy purpose can tempt aside. Bestow upon me understanding to know you, diligence to seek you, wisdom to find you, and faithfulness that finally may embrace you. **Amen.**

95. IN TIMES OF SUFFERING OR WEAKNESS

Dear Lord and Savior Jesus Christ: I hold up all my weakness to your strength, my failure to your faithfulness, my sinfulness to your perfection, my loneliness to your compassion, my little pains to your great agony on the Cross. I pray that you will cleanse me, strengthen me, guide me, so that in all ways my life may be lived as you would have it lived, without cowardice and for you alone. Show me how to live in true humility, true contrition, and true love. **Amen.**

96. FOR UNION WITH CHRIST *Anima Christi*

Soul of Christ, sanctify me. Body of Christ, save me. Blood of Christ, inebriate me. Water from the side of Christ, wash me. Passion of Christ, strengthen me. O good Jesus, hear me. Within thy wounds hide me. Permit me not to be separated from thee. From the wicked foe defend me. In the hour of my death call me, and bid me come to thee, that with thy saints I may praise thee for ever and ever. **Amen.**

97. PREPARATION FOR PERSONAL PRAYER

Holy Spirit, breath of God and fire of love, I cannot pray without your aid: Kindle in me the fire of your love, and illumine me with your light; that with a steadfast will and holy thoughts I may approach the Father in spirit and in truth; through Jesus Christ my Lord, who reigns with you and the Father in eternal union. **Amen.**

98. FOR THE ACCEPTANCE OF PRAYER

Heavenly Father, you have promised to hear what we ask in the Name of your Son: Accept and fulfill our petitions, we pray, not as we ask in our ignorance, nor as we deserve in our sinfulness, but as you know and love us in your Son Jesus Christ our Lord. **Amen.**

99. FOR THE ACCEPTANCE OF PRAYER

O Lord our God, accept the fervent prayers of your people; in the multitude of your mercies, look with compassion upon us and all who turn to you for help; for you are gracious, O lover of souls, and to you we give glory, Father, Son, and Holy Spirit, now and for ever. **Amen.**

100. FOR THE ANSWERING OF PRAYER

Almighty God, you have promised to hear the petitions of those who ask in the Name of your Son: Mercifully incline your ear to us as we make our prayers and supplications to you; and grant that what we ask faithfully, according to your will, we may obtain effectually, for the relief of our necessities and the setting forth of your glory; through Jesus Christ our Lord. **Amen.**

101. BEFORE THE READING OF SCRIPTURE

Blessed Lord, who caused all Holy Scriptures to be written for our learning: Grant us so to hear them, read, mark, learn, and inwardly digest them, that by patience and the comfort of your Holy Word we may embrace and ever hold fast the blessed hope of everlasting life, which you have given us in our Savior Jesus Christ; who lives and reigns with you and the Holy Spirit, one God, for ever and ever. **Amen.**

102. ON SUNDAYS

O God, you make us glad with the weekly remembrance of the glorious resurrection of your Son our Lord: Give us this day such blessing through our worship of you, that the week to come may be spent in your favor; through Jesus Christ our Lord. **Amen.**

103. PREPARATION FOR PUBLIC WORSHIP

Guide and direct us, O Lord, always and everywhere with your holy light, that we may discern with clear vision your presence among us, and partake with worthy intention of your divine mysteries. We ask this for Jesus Christ's sake. **Amen.**

104. BEFORE RECEIVING COMMUNION

Be present, be present, O Jesus, our great High Priest, as you were present with your disciples, and be known to us in the breaking of bread; who live and reign with the Father and the Holy Spirit, now and for ever. **Amen.**

105. AFTER RECEIVING COMMUNION

O Lord Jesus Christ, in this wonderful Sacrament you have given us a memorial of your passion: Grant us, we pray, so to venerate the sacred mysteries of your Body and Blood, that we may ever perceive within ourselves the fruit of your redemption; who live and reign with the Father and the Holy Spirit, one God, for ever and ever. **Amen.**

106. FOR SPIRITUAL COMMUNION

Dear Jesus, I believe that you are truly present in the Holy Sacrament. I love you above all things, and I desire to possess you within my soul. And since I cannot now receive you sacramentally, I beseech you to come spiritually into my heart. I unite myself to you, together with all your faithful people [gathered around every altar of your Church], and I embrace you with all the affections of my soul. Never permit me to be separated from you. **Amen.**

107. AFTER COMMUNION *Liturgy of St. Basil*

Finished and perfected is the mystery of thy dispensation to us, O Christ our God: For we have beheld the likeness of thy death, we have seen thy resurrection in the breaking of the bread, and we have partaken of thine inexhaustible and divine delights, of which do thou make us worthy, both now and in thy kingdom and unto the ages of ages. **Amen.**

108. AFTER PUBLIC WORSHIP

Grant, Almighty God, that the words we have heard this day with our ears may by your grace be grafted in our hearts, that they may bring forth in us the fruit of a righteous life, to the honor and praise of your Name; through Jesus Christ our Lord. **Amen.**

DEATH, THE DEPARTED, AND
THE COMMUNION OF SAINTS

109. FOR WATCHFULNESS — *Lancelot Andrewes*

Thou, who with thine own mouth hast told us that at midnight
the bridegroom shall come: Grant that the cry, "The bridegroom
cometh!" may sound evermore in our ears, that so we be never
unprepared to meet him, or forgetful of the souls for whom he
died, for whom we watch and pray. And save us, O Lord. **Amen.**

110. FOR JOY AT THE END OF LIFE — *Miles Coverdale*

Lord Jesus, be mindful of your promise. Think of us, your
servants, and when we shall depart, speak to our spirits these
loving words: "Today you shall be with me in joy." O Lord Jesus
Christ, remember us, your servants who trust in you, when our
tongues cannot speak, when the sight of our eyes fails, and when
our ears are stopped. Let our spirits always rejoice in you and be
joyful about our salvation, which you, through your death, have
purchased for us. **Amen.**

111. FOR AN ANNIVERSARY OF ONE DEPARTED

Almighty God, we remember this day before you your faithful
servant *N.*, and we pray that, having opened to *him* the gates of
larger life, you will receive *him* more and more into your joyful
service, that *he* may win, with you and your servants everywhere,
the eternal victory; through Jesus Christ our Lord. **Amen.**

112. THE COMMUNION OF SAINTS

O God of the spirits of all flesh, we praise and magnify thy holy
Name for all thy servants who have finished their course in thy
faith and fear [especially thy servant *N.*]; and we beseech thee

that, encouraged by their examples and strengthened by their fellowship, we also may be found meet to be partakers of the inheritance of the saints in light; through the merits of thy Son Jesus Christ our Lord. **Amen.**

113. THE COMMUNION OF SAINTS

O eternal Lord God, you hold all souls in life: Shed forth upon your whole Church in Paradise and on earth the bright beams of your light and heavenly comfort; and grant that we, following the good example of those who have loved and served you here and are now at rest, may enter with them into the fullness of your unending joy; through Jesus Christ our Lord. **Amen.**

114. FOR ALL FAITHFUL DEPARTED

Almighty God, with whom the souls of the faithful who have departed this life are in joy and felicity: We praise and magnify your holy Name for all your servants who have finished their course in your faith and fear; and we most humbly pray that, at the day of resurrection, we and all who are members of the mystical body of your Son may be set on his right hand, and hear his most joyful voice: "Come, you who are blessed by my Father, inherit the kingdom prepared for you from the foundation of the world." Grant this, O merciful Father, for the sake of Jesus Christ, our only Mediator and Advocate. **Amen.**

See also Additional Prayers in Burial of the Dead on pages 263-265

115. FOR THE COMING OF GOD'S KINGDOM

Hasten, O Father, the coming of your kingdom; and grant that we your servants, who now live by faith, may with joy behold your Son at his coming in glorious majesty; even Jesus Christ, our only Mediator and Advocate. **Amen.**

116. A LITANY OF THANKSGIVING

Let us give thanks to God our Father for all his gifts so freely bestowed upon us:

For the beauty and wonder of your creation, in earth and sky and sea,
> **We thank you, Lord.**

For our daily food and drink, our homes and families, and our friends,
> **We thank you, Lord.**

For minds to think, and hearts to love, and hands to serve,
> **We thank you, Lord.**

For health and strength to work, and time to rest and worship,
> **We thank you, Lord.**

For all who are patient in suffering and faithful in adversity,
> **We thank you, Lord.**

For all who earnestly seek after truth, and all who labor for justice,
> **We thank you, Lord.**

For all that is good and gracious in the lives of men and women, revealing the image of Christ,
> **We thank you, Lord.**

For the communion of saints, in all times and places,
> **We thank you, Lord.**

Above all, we give you thanks for the great mercies and promises given to us in Christ Jesus our Lord;
> **To him be praise and glory, with you, O Father,**
> **and the Holy Spirit, now and for ever. Amen.**

See also the General Thanksgiving on page 25 and A Litany of Thanksgiving for a Church on page 539

117. A THANKSGIVING PRAYER

Accept, O Lord, our thanks and praise for all that you have done for us. We thank you for the splendor of the whole creation, for the beauty of this world, for the wonder of life, and for the mystery of love. We thank you for the blessing of family and friends, and for the loving care which surrounds us on every side. We thank you for setting us at tasks that demand our best efforts, and for leading us to accomplishments that satisfy and delight us. We thank you also for those disappointments and failures that lead us to acknowledge our dependence on you alone. Above all, we thank you for your Son Jesus Christ; for the truth of his Word and the example of his life; for his steadfast obedience, by which he overcame temptation; for his dying, through which he conquered death; and for his rising to life again, in which we are raised to the life of your kingdom. Grant us the gift of your Spirit, that we may know Christ and make him known; and through him, at all times and in all places, may give thanks to you in all things. **Amen.**

118. FOR THE MISSION OF THE CHURCH

Almighty God, you sent your Son Jesus Christ to reconcile the world to yourself: We praise and bless you for those whom you have sent in the power of the Spirit to preach the Gospel to all nations. We thank you that in all parts of the earth a community of love has been gathered together by their prayers and labors, and that in every place your servants call upon your Name; for the kingdom and the power and the glory are yours, for ever and ever. **Amen.**

119. FOR THE HARVEST

Most gracious God, by whose knowledge the depths are broken up and the clouds drop down the dew: We yield you hearty thanks and praise for the return of seed-time and harvest, for the increase of the ground and the gathering in of its fruits, and for all the other blessings your merciful providence has bestowed upon this nation and people. And, we pray, give us a just sense of these great mercies, that we may walk before you in humility, holiness, and obedience all our days; through Jesus Christ our Lord, to whom, with you and the Holy Spirit, be all glory and honor, world without end. **Amen.**

120. FOR THE BEAUTY OF THE EARTH

We give you thanks, most gracious God, for the beauty of earth and sky and sea; for the richness of mountains, plains, and rivers; for the wonder of your creatures, large and small; and for all the loveliness that surrounds us. We praise you for these good gifts, and pray that we may safeguard them for our posterity. Grant that we may continue to grow in our grateful enjoyment of your abundant creation, to the honor and glory of your Name, now and for ever. **Amen.**

121. FOR THE DIVERSITY OF RACES AND CULTURES

O God, who created all peoples in your image: We thank you for the diversity of races and cultures in this world. Show us your presence in those who differ from us, and enrich our lives with their fellowship, until our knowledge of your love is made perfect in our love for all your children; through Jesus Christ our Lord. **Amen.**

122. FOR MILITARY VETERANS

O Judge of the nations, we thank you with grateful hearts for the men and women of our country who in the day of decision ventured much for the liberties we now enjoy. Grant that we may not rest until all the people of this land share the benefits of true freedom and gladly accept its disciplines. This we ask in the Name of Jesus Christ our Lord. **Amen.**

123. FOR DELIVERANCE FROM PERIL

Almighty God, our strong tower of defense in time of trouble:
We offer you praise and heartfelt thanks for our deliverance
from the dangers which lately surrounded us [and for your
gracious gift of peace]. We confess that your goodness alone
has preserved us; and we ask you still to continue your mercies
toward us, that we may always know and acknowledge you as
our Savior and mighty Deliverer; through Jesus Christ our Lord.
Amen.

124. FOR THE RESTORATION OF HEALTH

Almighty God and heavenly Father, we bless and praise your
Name on behalf of your servant *N.*, and we give you humble
thanks that you have been pleased to deliver *him* from sickness.
Grant, O gracious Father, that by your help *he* may live in
this world according to your will, and be made a partaker of
everlasting glory in the life to come; through Jesus Christ our
Lord. **Amen.**

125. FOR THE SAINTS AND FAITHFUL DEPARTED

We give thanks to you, O Lord our God, for all your servants
and witnesses of time past: for Abraham, the father of believers,
and Sarah his wife; for Moses, the lawgiver, and Aaron, the
priest; for Miriam and Joshua, Deborah and Gideon, and
Samuel with Hannah his mother; for David, King over Israel;
for Isaiah and all the prophets; for Mary, the mother of our
Lord; for Peter and Paul and all the apostles; for Mary and
Martha, and Mary Magdalene; for Stephen, the first martyr, and
all the martyrs and saints in every age and in every land. In your
mercy, O Lord our God, give us, as you gave to them, the hope
of salvation and the promise of eternal life; through Jesus Christ
our Lord, the first-born of many from the dead. **Amen.**

THE CALENDAR
of the CHRISTIAN YEAR

AN INTRODUCTION

The Christian Year consists of two cycles of holy days. The first is the Paschal Cycle, which follows the lunar calendar and identifies the first Sunday after the full moon that falls on or after March 21 as Easter Day. (Easter Day cannot occur before March 22 or after April 25.) The season of Lent precedes Eastertide and the Season after Pentecost follows it. The second cycle, the Incarnation Cycle, follows the solar calendar and places our Lord's birth on December 25 (Christmas Day) with the season of Advent preceding it. The season of Epiphany follows the twelve days of the Christmas season (Christmastide.)

SUNDAYS

The sequence of the Sundays of the Calendar depends on the date of Easter, because every Sunday is a celebration of our Lord's resurrection from the dead. Nevertheless, Sundays also reflect the character of the seasons in which they are set. Following ancient Jewish tradition, the celebration of any Sunday begins at sundown on the Saturday that precedes it. Therefore at Evening Prayer on Saturdays (other than Holy Days), the Collect appointed for the ensuing Sunday is used.

Easter Day	Christmas Day *December 25*
Ascension Day	The Epiphany *January 6*
The Day of Pentecost	All Saints' Day *November 1*
Trinity Sunday	

These feasts take precedence over any other day or observance. All Saints' Day may also be observed on the Sunday following November 1, in addition to its observance on the fixed date. In Canada, when Remembrance Day observances fall on the first Sunday of November, All Saints' Day may be observed on the preceding Sunday.

HOLY DAYS

The Holy Days, traditionally called Red-Letter Days, observed in this church, in addition to the Principal Feasts, are the following:

The Circumcision and Holy Name *January 1*
The Presentation of Christ in the Temple *February 2*
Joseph, the Guardian of Jesus *March 19*
The Annunciation *March 25*
The Feasts of the Apostles
The Feasts of the Evangelists
The Visitation *May 31*
The Nativity of John the Baptist *June 24*
Mary Magdalene *July 22*
The Transfiguration *August 6*
The Virgin Mary *August 15*
Holy Cross Day *September 14*
Holy Michael and All Angels *September 29*
James of Jerusalem *October 23*
Stephen, Deacon and Martyr *December 26*
The Holy Innocents *December 28*

Any of these feasts that fall on a Sunday, other than in Advent, Lent, and Easter, may be observed on that Sunday or transferred to the nearest following weekday.

The last three Sundays before Lent may be observed as Septuagesima, Sexagesima, and Quinquagesima.

No holy day or observance can replace the fixed propers for Ash Wednesday, Holy Week, or Easter Week.

DAYS OF DISCIPLINE, DENIAL, AND SPECIAL PRAYER

Ash Wednesday, the first day of Lent, and Good Friday, the day of our Lord's Crucifixion, are traditionally days of special devotion and total abstinence. Maundy Thursday is observed with rites recalling the Last Supper and betrayal at Gethsemane.

The weekdays of Lent and every Friday of the year (outside the 12 Days of Christmas and the 50 days of Eastertide) are encouraged as days of fasting. Ember Days and Rogation Days may also be kept in this way.

Fasting, in addition to reduced consumption, normally also includes prayer, self-examination, and acts of mercy.

Ember Days are set aside for prayers for those called to Holy Orders, and occur on the following Wednesdays, Fridays, and Saturdays:

After St. Lucy's Day *December 13*
After the First Sunday in Lent
After the Day of Pentecost
After Holy Cross Day *September 14*

Rogation Days are the three days preceding Ascension Day, especially devoted to asking for God's blessing on agriculture and industry.

National Days with proper lessons are:

Memorial Day *(United States on the Monday closest to May 28)*

Canada Day *(Canada on July 1)*

Independence Day *(United States on July 4)*

Thanksgiving Day *(Canada on the second Monday in October;
United States on the fourth Thursday in November)*

Remembrance Day *(Canada on November 11)*

COMMEMORATIONS

The Book of Common Prayer of 1662 appointed days of optional commemoration (Black Letter Days). In this edition of the Book of Common Prayer, two categories of optional commemorations are presented: Anglican and Ecumenical. These commemorations may be transferred or observed as local needs dictate. Collects and Lessons are offered in nine categories: Martyr, Missionary or Evangelist, Pastor, Teacher of the Faith, Monastic or Religious, Ecumenist, Reformer of the Church, Renewer of Society, and any Saint. The daily psalms and readings at Morning and Evening prayer are not usually superseded by these commemorations.

Those preparing weekday liturgies are encouraged to limit the number of commemorations, especially in Advent or Lent, in order that the spirit of the season be maintained.

CALENDAR

JANUARY			
DAY	RED-LETTER HOLY DAYS	OPTIONAL COMMEMORATIONS ANGLICAN	OPTIONAL COMMEMORATIONS ECUMENICAL
1	The Circumcision and Holy Name of Our Lord Jesus Christ		
2		Vedanayagam Samuel Azariah, *Bishop in South India, Evangelist*, 1945	
3			
4			
5			
6	The Epiphany of Our Lord Jesus Christ		
7			
8			
9			
10		William Laud, *Archbishop of Canterbury, Martyr*, 1645	
11			
12			
13			Hilary of Poitiers, *Bishop and Teacher of the Faith*, 367
14		Kentigern, *Missionary to Strathclyde and Cumbria*, 603	
15			

DAY	RED-LETTER HOLY DAYS	OPTIONAL COMMEMORATIONS ANGLICAN	OPTIONAL COMMEMORATIONS ECUMENICAL
		JANUARY	
16			
17			Anthony, *Hermit in Egypt*, 356
18	Confession of Peter the Apostle		
19		Wulfstan, *Bishop of Worcester*, 1095	
20			Fabian, *Bishop of Rome and Martyr*, 250
21			Agnes, *Martyr at Rome*, 304
22			Vincent, *Deacon of Saragossa, Martyr*, 304
23			
24			
25	Conversion of Paul the Apostle		
26			Timothy and Titus, *Companions of Paul the Apostle*
27			Lydia, Dorcas, and Phoebe, *Helpers of the Apostles*
28			Thomas Aquinas, *Friar, Priest, and Teacher of the Faith*, 1274
29		Lesslie Newbigin, *Bishop and Ecumenist*, 1998	
30		Charles, *King and Martyr*, 1649	
31		Samuel Shoemaker, *Priest and Renewer of Society*, 1963	

FEBRUARY

DAY	RED-LETTER HOLY DAYS	OPTIONAL COMMEMORATIONS ANGLICAN	OPTIONAL COMMEMORATIONS ECUMENICAL
1		Brigid, *Abbess of Kildare*, 523	
2	The Presentation of Our Lord Jesus Christ in the Temple		
3			Anskar, *Bishop and Missionary to Denmark and Sweden*, 865
4			Cornelius the Centurion
5			Martyrs of Japan, 1597
6			
7			
8			
9			
10			Scholastica, *Abbess*, 543
11			
12			
13		Absalom Jones, *First African-American Priest*, 1818	
14			Cyril and Methodius, *Apostles to the Slavs*, 869, 885
15		Thomas Bray, *Priest and Missionary, founder of SPG and SPCK*, 1730	
16			
17		Janani Luwum, *Archbishop of Uganda and Martyr*, 1977	
18			Martin Luther, *Reformer of the Church*, 1546

DAY	RED-LETTER HOLY DAYS	OPTIONAL COMMEMORATIONS ANGLICAN	OPTIONAL COMMEMORATIONS ECUMENICAL
	FEBRUARY		
19			
20			
21			William "Billy" Graham, *Evangelist*, 2018
22			
23			Polycarp, *Bishop of Smyrna, Martyr*, 156
24	Matthias the Apostle		
25			
26			
27		George Herbert, *Priest and Poet*, 1633	
28			John Cassian, *Monk and Teacher of the Faith*, 453
	MARCH		
1		David, *Bishop and Apostle of Wales*, 601	
2		Chad, *Bishop of Lichfield and Missionary*, 672	
3		John and Charles Wesley, *Priests and Reformers of the Church*, 1791, 1788	
4			
5			
6			
7			Perpetua and Her Companions, *Martyrs at Carthage*, 203
8		Felix, *Bishop and Missionary to the Angles*, 647	

		MARCH	
DAY	RED-LETTER HOLY DAYS	OPTIONAL COMMEMORATIONS ANGLICAN	OPTIONAL COMMEMORATIONS ECUMENICAL
9			
10		Robert Machray, *First Primate of Canada*, 1904	
11			
12			Gregory the Great, *Bishop of Rome and Teacher of the Faith*, 604
13			
14			
15			
16			
17		Patrick, *Bishop and Apostle to the Irish*, 461	
18			Cyril, *Bishop of Jerusalem and Teacher of the Faith*, 386
19	**Joseph,** *Husband of the Virgin Mary and Guardian of Jesus*		
20		Cuthbert, *Bishop-Abbot of Lindisfarne and Missionary*, 687	
21		Thomas Cranmer, *Archbishop of Canterbury and Martyr*, 1556	
22		James DeKoven, *Priest*, 1879	
23			Gregory the Illuminator, *Missionary to Armenia*, 333
24			

		MARCH	
DAY	RED-LETTER HOLY DAYS	OPTIONAL COMMEMORATIONS ANGLICAN	OPTIONAL COMMEMORATIONS ECUMENICAL
25	The Annunciation of our Lord Jesus Christ to the Virgin Mary		
26			
27		Charles Henry Brent, *Bishop and Missionary to the Philippines*, 1929	
28			
29		John Keble, *Priest and Reformer of the Church*, 1866	
30			
31		John Donne, *Priest and Poet*, 1631	
		APRIL	
1		Frederick Denison Maurice, *Priest and Renewer of Society*, 1872	
2		Henry Budd, *First Native Priest in Canada*, 1850	
3		James Lloyd Breck, *Priest and Missionary*, 1879	
4			Martin Luther King, Jr., *Renewer of Society*, 1968
5			
6			
7			Tikhon, *Bishop and Ecumenist*, 1925
8		William Augustus Muhlenberg, *Priest, Reformer of the Church, and Renewer of Society*, 1877	

		APRIL	
DAY	RED-LETTER HOLY DAYS	OPTIONAL COMMEMORATIONS ANGLICAN	OPTIONAL COMMEMORATIONS ECUMENICAL
9			
10		William Law, *Priest and Teacher of the Faith,* 1761	
11		George Augustus Selwyn, *Bishop and Missionary to New Zealand,* 1878	
12			
13			
14			
15			
16			
17			
18			
19		Alphege, *Archbishop of Canterbury and Martyr,* 1012	
20			
21		Anselm, *Archbishop of Canterbury and Teacher of the Faith,* 1109	
22			
23			George, *Martyr,* c. 304
24		Arthur Michael Ramsey, *Archbishop of Canterbury, Ecumenist, and Teacher of the Faith,* 1988	
25	Mark the Evangelist		
26			
27			
28			

DAY	RED-LETTER HOLY DAYS	OPTIONAL COMMEMORATIONS ANGLICAN	OPTIONAL COMMEMORATIONS ECUMENICAL
		APRIL	
29			Catherine of Siena, *Reformer of the Church*, 1380
30			
		MAY	
1	Philip and James, *Apostles*		
2			Athanasius, *Bishop of Alexandria and Teacher of the Faith*, 373
3			
4			
5			
6			
7			
8		Julian of Norwich, *Anchoress*, c. 1417	
9			Gregory of Nazianzus, *Bishop of Constantinople and Teacher of the Faith*, 389
10			
11			
12			
13			
14			
15			Pachomius, *Abbot and Organizer of Monasticism*, 346
16		The Martyrs of the Sudan, 2011	
17			

MAY			
DAY	RED-LETTER HOLY DAYS	OPTIONAL COMMEMORATIONS ANGLICAN	OPTIONAL COMMEMORATIONS ECUMENICAL
18			
19		Dunstan, *Archbishop of Canterbury and Reformer of the Church*, 988	
20		Alcuin, *Deacon and Abbot of Tours*, 804	
21			Helena, *Mother of Constantine and Protector of the Holy Places*, 330
22			
23			
24		Jackson Kemper, *First Missionary Bishop in the United States*, 1870	
25		Bede the Venerable, *Priest and Monk of Jarrow, Teacher of the Faith*, 735	
26		Augustine, *First Archbishop of Canterbury and Missionary*, 605	
27			John Calvin, *Reformer of the Church*, 1564
28			
29			
30		Josephine Butler, *Renewer of Society*, 1906	
31	The Visitation of the Virgin Mary to Elizabeth and Zechariah		

		JUNE	
DAY	RED-LETTER HOLY DAYS	OPTIONAL COMMEMORATIONS ANGLICAN	OPTIONAL COMMEMORATIONS ECUMENICAL
1			Justin, *Teacher of the Faith and Martyr at Rome,* c. 165
2			Blandina and Her Companions, *Martyrs at Lyons,* 177
3		The Martyrs of Uganda, 1886, 1977	
4			John XXIII, *Bishop of Rome, Ecumenist, and Reformer of the Church,* 1963
5		Boniface, *Archbishop of Mainz, Missionary to the Germans, and Martyr,* 754	
6		William Grant Broughton, *Bishop and Missionary to Australia,* 1853	
7			
8		Thomas Ken, *Bishop of Bath and Wells, Non-juror,* 1711	
9		Columba, *Abbot of Iona and Missionary to the Scots,* 597	
10			Ephrem of Edessa, *Deacon and Teacher of the Faith,* 373
11	**Barnabas the Apostle**		
12			
13			
14			Basil the Great, *Bishop of Caesarea and Teacher of the Faith,* 379
15		Evelyn Underhill, *Teacher of the Faith,* 1941	

DAY	RED-LETTER HOLY DAYS	OPTIONAL COMMEMORATIONS ANGLICAN	OPTIONAL COMMEMORATIONS ECUMENICAL
		JUNE	
16			
17			
18		Bernard Mizeki, *Catechist and Martyr in Rhodesia,* 1896	
19		Sundar Singh, *Evangelist in India and Teacher of the Faith,* 1929	
20			
21			
22		Alban, *First Martyr of Britain,* c. 250	
23			
24	The Nativity of John the Baptist		
25			
26			
27			Cyril of Alexandria, *Bishop and Teacher of the Faith,* 444
28			Irenaeus, *Bishop of Lyons and Teacher of the Faith,* 200
29	Peter and Paul, *Apostles*		
30			
		JULY	
1			*Canada Day*
2			
3			
4			*Independence Day (USA)*
5			

DAY	RED-LETTER HOLY DAYS	OPTIONAL COMMEMORATIONS ANGLICAN	OPTIONAL COMMEMORATIONS ECUMENICAL
		JULY	
6			
7			
8			
9			
10			
11			Benedict of Nursia, *Abbot and Founder of the Benedictine Order*, c. 550
12			Nathan Soderblom, *Archbishop of Uppsala and Ecumenist*, 1931
13			
14			Bonaventure, *Friar, Bishop, and Teacher of the Faith*, 1274
15			Olga and Vladimir, *Patrons of the Church in Russia*, 969, 1016
16			
17		William White, *Bishop of Pennsylvania and First Presiding Bishop of the Church in the USA*, 1836	
18			Macrina, *Nun and Teacher of the Faith*, 379
19			Gregory, *Bishop of Nyssa and Teacher of the Faith*, 396
20			Margaret of Antioch, *Martyr*, 4th c.
21			
22	Mary Magdalene		
23			

174

DAY	RED-LETTER HOLY DAYS	OPTIONAL COMMEMORATIONS ANGLICAN	OPTIONAL COMMEMORATIONS ECUMENICAL
		JULY	
24			Thomas à Kempis, *Priest and Teacher of the Faith,* 1471
25	James the Elder, *Apostle*		
26			The Parents of the Virgin Mary
27		William Reed Huntington, *Priest and Ecumenist,* 1909	
28			
29			Lazarus, Mary, and Martha of Bethany, *Companions of our Lord*
30		William Wilberforce, *Renewer of Society,* 1833	
31			
		AUGUST	
1			Joseph of Arimathea
2			
3			
4			
5		Oswald, *King of Northumbria and Martyr,* 642	
6	The Transfiguration of Our Lord Jesus Christ		
7		John Mason Neale, *Priest and Reformer of the Church,* 1866	
8			Dominic, *Priest and Friar,* 1221

	AUGUST		
DAY	RED-LETTER HOLY DAYS	OPTIONAL COMMEMORATIONS ANGLICAN	OPTIONAL COMMEMORATIONS ECUMENICAL
9		Mary Sumner, *Founder of the Mothers' Union and Renewer of Society*, 1921	
10			Laurence, *Deacon and Martyr at Rome*, 258
11			Clare, *Abbess of Assisi*, 1253
12		Charles Inglis, *First Bishop of Canada*, 1787	
13		Jeremy Taylor, *Bishop of Down and Connor, Teacher of the Faith*, 1667	
14			Roger Schutz, *Monk of Taizé and Ecumenist*, 2005
15	The Virgin Mary, *Mother of Our Lord Jesus Christ*		
16			
17			
18			
19			
20			Bernard, *Abbot of Clairvaux and Teacher of the Faith*, 1153
21		Jonathan Myrick Daniels, *Martyr*, 1965	
22			
23			
24	Bartholomew the Apostle		
25			Louis, *King of France*, 1270
26			

DAY	RED-LETTER HOLY DAYS	OPTIONAL COMMEMORATIONS ANGLICAN	OPTIONAL COMMEMORATIONS ECUMENICAL
		AUGUST	
27			Monica, *Mother of Augustine of Hippo,* 387
28			Augustine, *Bishop of Hippo and Teacher of the Faith,* 430
29			The Beheading of John the Baptist
30		Charles Chapman Grafton, *Bishop of Fond du Lac and Ecumenist,* 1912	
31		Aidan, *Abbot-Bishop of Lindisfarne, Missionary to Northumbria,* 651	
		SEPTEMBER	
1			
2		The Martyrs of Papua New Guinea, 1901 and 1942	
3			
4		Birinus, *Bishop of Dorchester and Evangelist to Wessex,* 650	
5			Mother Teresa of Calcutta, *Renewer of Society,* 1997
6		Alan Gardiner, *Missionary and Founder of SAMS,* 1851	
7		Hannah More, *Renewer of Society and Founder of Sunday Schools,* 1833	
8			
9		Constance and her Companions, *Martyrs of Memphis,* 1878	
10		Alexander Crummell, *Priest and Missionary to Liberia,* 1898	

SEPTEMBER			
DAY	RED–LETTER HOLY DAYS	OPTIONAL COMMEMORATIONS ANGLICAN	OPTIONAL COMMEMORATIONS ECUMENICAL
11			
12		John Henry Hobart, *Bishop of New York and Reformer of the Church*, 1830	
13			John Chrysostom, *Bishop of Constantinople and Teacher of the Faith*, 407
14	**Holy Cross Day**		
15			Cyprian, *Bishop of Carthage and Martyr*, 258
16		Ninian, *Bishop of Galloway and Missionary to the Picts*, 432	
17		Edward Bouverie Pusey, *Priest and Teacher of the Faith*, 1882	
18			
19		Theodore of Tarsus, *Archbishop of Canterbury*, 690	
20		John Coleridge Patteson, *Bishop of Melanesia,* and his Companions, *Martyrs*, 1871	
21	**Matthew,** *Apostle and Evangelist*		
22			
23			
24			
25			Sergius, *Monk and Reformer of the Church in Russia*, 1392
26		Lancelot Andrewes, *Bishop of Winchester and Teacher of the Faith*, 1626	

		SEPTEMBER	
DAY	RED-LETTER HOLY DAYS	OPTIONAL COMMEMORATIONS ANGLICAN	OPTIONAL COMMEMORATIONS ECUMENICAL
27		Wilson Carlile, *Evangelist and Founder of the Church Army*, 1942	
28			
29	Holy Michael and All Angels		
30			Jerome, *Monk of Bethlehem and Translator of the Bible*, 420
		OCTOBER	
1			Remigius, *Bishop of Reims and Missionary to the Franks*, 533
2			
3		George Bell, *Advocate for the Confessing Church, Bishop and Ecumenist*, 1958	
4			Francis of Assisi, *Friar and Deacon, Reformer of the Church*, 1226
5			
6		William Tyndale, *Priest, Translator of the Bible, and Martyr*, 1536	
7			
8			
9		Robert Grosseteste, *Bishop of Lincoln*, 1253	
10		Paulinus, *Bishop of York and Missionary*, 644	
11			Philip, *Deacon and Evangelist*

OCTOBER

DAY	RED-LETTER HOLY DAYS	OPTIONAL COMMEMORATIONS ANGLICAN	OPTIONAL COMMEMORATIONS ECUMENICAL
12		Cecil Frances Alexander, *Hymn-writer and Teacher of the Faith*, 1895	
13		Edward the Confessor, *King of England*, 1066	
14		Samuel Isaac Joseph Schereschewsky, *Bishop of Shanghai*, 1906	
15			Teresa of Ávila, *Nun and Reformer of the Church*, 1582
16		Hugh Latimer and Nicholas Ridley, *Bishops and Martyrs*, 1555	
17			Ignatius, *Bishop of Antioch and Martyr*, ca. 115
18	Luke the Evangelist and Companion of Paul		
19		Henry Martyn, *Priest and Missionary to India and Persia*, 1812	
20			
21			
22			
23	James of Jerusalem, *Bishop and Martyr, Brother of Our Lord*		
24			
25			

OCTOBER

DAY	RED-LETTER HOLY DAYS	OPTIONAL COMMEMORATIONS ANGLICAN	OPTIONAL COMMEMORATIONS ECUMENICAL
26		Alfred the Great, *King of the West Saxons and Reformer of the Church*, 899	
27			
28	Simon and Jude, *Apostles*		
29		James Hannington, *Bishop of Eastern Equatorial Africa*, and his Companions, *Martyrs*, 1885	
30			
31			

NOVEMBER

1	All Saints' Day		
2			Commemoration of the Faithful Departed
3		Richard Hooker, *Priest and Teacher of the Faith*, 1600	
4			
5			Elizabeth and Zechariah, *Parents of John the Baptist*
6		William Temple, *Archbishop of Canterbury and Teacher of the Faith*, 1944	
7			Willibrord, *Archbishop of Utrecht and Missionary to Frisia*, 739
8			
9			
10			Leo the Great, *Bishop of Rome and Teacher of the Faith*, 461

		NOVEMBER	
DAY	RED-LETTER HOLY DAYS	OPTIONAL COMMEMORATIONS ANGLICAN	OPTIONAL COMMEMORATIONS ECUMENICAL
11			Martin, *Bishop of Tours*, 397
12			
13		Charles Simeon, *Priest and Evangelist*, 1836	
14		Consecration of Samuel Seabury, *First Bishop in the United States*, 1784	
15			Herman, *Monk and Missionary to the Native Alaskans*, 1837
16		Margaret, *Queen of Scotland, Reformer of the Church, and Renewer of Society*, 1093	
17		Hugh, *Bishop of Lincoln and Renewer of Society*, 1200	
18			Elizabeth of Hungary, *Renewer of Society*, 1231
19		Hilda, *Abbess of Whitby*, 680	
20		Edmund, *King of East Anglia and Martyr*, 870	
21			
22			Cecilia, *Martyr at Rome*, c. 230
23			Clement, *Bishop of Rome and Martyr*, c. 100
24			
25			Catherine of Alexandria, *Martyr*, c. 305
26			
27			
28			

DAY	RED-LETTER HOLY DAYS	OPTIONAL COMMEMORATIONS ANGLICAN	OPTIONAL COMMEMORATIONS ECUMENICAL
		NOVEMBER	
29		Clive Staples Lewis, *Teacher of the Faith*, 1963	
30	**Andrew the Apostle**		
		DECEMBER	
1		Nicholas Ferrar, *Deacon and Founder of the Little Gidding Community*, 1637	
2		Channing Moore Williams, *Missionary Bishop in China and Japan*, 1910	
3			
4			John of Damascus, *Priest and Teacher of the Faith*, 760
5			Clement of Alexandria, *Priest and Teacher of the Faith*, 210
6			Nicholas, *Bishop of Myra*, c.326
7			Ambrose, *Bishop of Milan and Teacher of the Faith*, 397
8		Richard Baxter, *Pastor and Teacher of the Faith*, 1691	
9			
10			
11			
12			
13			Lucy, *Martyr at Syracuse*, 304
14			
15			

DECEMBER

DAY	RED-LETTER HOLY DAYS	OPTIONAL COMMEMORATIONS ANGLICAN	OPTIONAL COMMEMORATIONS ECUMENICAL
16		*O Sapientia** O Wisdom from on high	
17		*O Adonai* O Lord of Might	
18		*O Radix Jesse* O Root of Jesse	
19		*O Clavis David* O Key of David	
20		*O Oriens* O Dayspring	
21	Thomas the Apostle	*O Rex Gentium* O Desire of Nations	
22		*O Emmanuel* O Come, Emmanuel	
23		*O Virgo Virginum* O Virgin of Virgins	
24			
25	The Nativity of our Lord Jesus Christ *Christmas*		
26	Stephen, *Deacon and Martyr*		
27	John, *Apostle and Evangelist*		
28	The Holy Innocents		
29		Thomas Becket, *Archbishop of Canterbury, Martyr*, 1170	
30			
31		John Wyclif, *Priest and Translator of the Bible into English*, 1384	

* *These traditional Advent antiphons are the basis for the hymn, "O Come, O Come, Emmanuel."*

DATE	MORNING PRAYER PSALMS	EVENING PRAYER PSALMS
1	1, 2, 3, 4, 5	6, 7, 8
2	9, 10, 11	12, 13, 14
3	15, 16, 17	18
4	19, 20, 21	22, 23
5	24, 25, 26	27, 28, 29
6	30, 31	32, 33, 34
7	35, 36	37
8	38, 39, 40	41, 42, 43
9	44, 45, 46	47, 48, 49
10	50, 51, 52	53, 54, 55
11	56, 57, 58	59, 60, 61
12	62, 63, 64	65, 66, 67
13	68	69, 70
14	71, 72	73, 74
15	75, 76, 77	78
16	79, 80, 81	82, 83, 84, 85
17	86, 87, 88	89
18	90, 91, 92	93, 94
19	95, 96, 97	98, 99, 100, 101
20	102, 103	104
21	105	106
22	107	108, 109
23	110, 111, 112, 113	114, 115
24	116, 117, 118	119:1-32
25	119:33-72	119:73-104
26	119:105-144	119:145-176
27	120, 121, 122, 123, 124, 125	126, 127, 128, 129, 130, 131
28	132, 133, 134, 135	136, 137, 138
29	139, 140	141, 142, 143
30	144, 145, 146	147, 148, 149, 150

If there is a 31st day of the month, psalms are chosen from among the Songs of Ascents (120 to 134).

The principle adopted at the Reformation was that "the whole of Holy Scripture (or the greatest part thereof)" should be read each year. This cycle of lessons is based on that principle.

The first lesson is normally taken from the Old Testament or the Apocrypha. The Old Testament is read in its entirety once each year (with the exception of a few passages in Leviticus, Numbers, Joshua, Judges, Ezra, Nehemiah, Ezekiel, and the majority of Chronicles). These readings may be shortened if necessary, as long as the plain sense of the text is not lost. The dagger symbol (†) indicates a way to abbreviate a longer chapter if desired. The Gospels and Acts are read in their entirety twice each year, at Morning Prayer during the first part of the year, at Evening Prayer during the second part of the year. The Epistles are read twice each year in the opposite pattern, except for the Revelation to John, which is read only once, during the Advent season. Less of the Apocrypha has been included than in the 1662 *Book of Common Prayer*; however, select passages have been retained, in keeping with the classic Anglican principle that "the Church doth read [these books] for example of life and instruction of manners; but yet doth it not apply them to establish any doctrine" (Article VI of the Thirty-Nine Articles).

In general, readings move continuously through books of the Bible, interrupted only by Holy Days. For most Holy Days a single proper lesson is included, usually in Morning Prayer. For major feasts of our Lord, two proper lessons are included. The Holy Days connected to the date of Easter (Ash Wednesday, Maundy Thursday, Good Friday, Holy Saturday, Easter Day, Ascension, and Pentecost) have a variable calendar date year to year. Proper readings for these days are provided in additional tables in the midst of the lectionary, and are indicated at the earliest possible date with a double dagger (‡).

If Morning Prayer is the principal liturgy on a Sunday, the psalms and lessons appointed for the day should be replaced with the psalm and two of the lessons from the SUNDAY, HOLY DAY, AND COMMEMORATION LECTIONARY. On other Holy Days, the psalm and lessons from the SUNDAY, HOLY DAY, AND COMMEMORATION LECTIONARY may be used, if those lessons are not to be used at a celebration of the Eucharist on that day.

When a Lesson begins with a pronoun, the reader should substitute the appropriate noun.

Readings from the Apocrypha are in italics. It is appropriate to conclude readings from the Apocrypha with "Here ends the Reading." Should an alternate reading be desired to replace the Apocrypha, the reading appointed as the first lesson of the other Office for that day may be divided between the two Offices.

This Daily Office Lectionary may be adapted for use in a two-year cycle (indicated by I and II in the monthly headings) by reading only the two lessons appointed for Morning Prayer in odd-numbered years (e.g., 2019) and the two lessons appointed for Evening Prayer in even-numbered years (e.g., 2020). The two lessons each day may be divided across the two Offices. In this way, the New Testament will be read through once each year, and the Old Testament will be read through in two years.

	MORNING PRAYER		60 DAY PSALTER—MP
DATE	FIRST LESSON	SECOND LESSON	
1 *Circ. & Name*	Gen 1	John 1:1-28	1, 2
2	Gen 2	John 1:29-*end*	5, 6
3	Gen 3	John 2	9
4	Gen 4	John 3:1-21	8, 11
5	Gen 5	John 3:22-*end*	12, 13, 14
6 *Epiphany*	Gen 6	Matt 2:1-12	96, 97
7	Gen 7	John 4:1-26	18:1-20ᵛ
8	Gen 8	John 4:27-*end*	19
9	Gen 9	John 5:1-24	22
10	Gen 10 † 1-9,15-22,30-32	John 5:25-*end*	25
11	Gen 11 † 1-9,27-32	John 6:1-21	26, 28
12	Gen 12	John 6:22-40	29, 30
13	Gen 13	John 6:41-*end*	34
14	Gen 14	John 7:1-24	32, 36
15	Gen 15	John 7:25-52	37:1-17ᵛ
16	Gen 16	John 7:53—8:30	40
17	Gen 17	John 8:31-*end*	42, 43
18 *Conf. Peter*	Gen 18	Matt 16:13-20	45
19	Gen 19 † 1-29	John 9	47, 48
20	Gen 20	John 10:1-21	50
21	Gen 21 † 1-21	John 10:22-*end*	52, 53, 54
22	Gen 22	John 11:1-44	56, 57
23	Gen 23	John 11:45-*end*	59
24	Gen 24 † 1-28,53-58	John 12:1-19	61, 62
25 *Conv. Paul*	Acts 9:1-22	John 12:20-*end*	68:1-18
26	Gen 25 † 7-11,19-34	John 13	69:1-18ᵛ
27	Gen 26 † 1-25	John 14:1-14	66
28	Gen 27 † 1-13,18-36,39-40	John 14:15-*end*	71
29	Gen 28	John 15:1-17	74
30	Gen 29 † 1-28	John 15:18-*end*	75, 76
31	Gen 30 † 1-2,22-43	John 16:1-15	78:1-18ᵛ

† *Optional abbreviation*

60 DAY PSALTER—EP	EVENING PRAYER		
	DATE	FIRST LESSON	SECOND LESSON
3, 4	**1** *Circ. & Name*	Gal 1	Luke 2:8-21
7	**2**	Jer 1	Gal 2
10	**3**	Jer 2 † 1-22	Gal 3
15, 16	**4**	Jer 3	Gal 4
17	**5**	Jer 4	Gal 5
67, 72	**6** *Epiphany*	Jer 5	John 2:1-12
18:21-52ᵛ	**7**	Jer 6	Gal 6
20, 21	**8**	Jer 7 † 1-28,34	1 Thess 1
23, 24	**9**	Jer 8	1 Thess 2:1-16
27	**10**	Jer 9	1 Thess 2:17—3 *end*
31	**11**	Jer 10	1 Thess 4:1-12
33	**12**	Jer 11	1 Thess 4:13—5:11
35	**13**	Jer 12	1 Thess 5:12-*end*
38	**14**	Jer 13	2 Thess 1
37:18-41ᵛ	**15**	Jer 14	2 Thess 2
39, 41	**16**	Jer 15	2 Thess 3
44	**17**	Jer 16	1 Cor 1:1-25
46	**18** *Conf. Peter*	Jer 17	1 Cor 1:26—2 *end*
49	**19**	Jer 18	1 Cor 3
51	**20**	Jer 19	1 Cor 4:1-17
55	**21**	Jer 20	1 Cor 4:18—5 *end*
58, 60	**22**	Jer 21	1 Cor 6
63, 64	**23**	Jer 22	1 Cor 7
65, 67	**24**	Jer 23 † 1-9,16-18,21-40	1 Cor 8
68:19-36ᵛ	**25** *Conv. Paul*	Jer 24	1 Cor 9
69:19-37ᵛ	**26**	Jer 25 † 1-19,26-31	1 Cor 10
70, 72	**27**	Jer 26	1 Cor 11
73	**28**	Jer 27	1 Cor 12
77	**29**	Jer 28	1 Cor 13
79, 82	**30**	Jer 29 † 1-14,24-32	1 Cor 14:1-19
78:19-40ᵛ	**31**	Jer 30	1 Cor 14:20-*end*

† *Optional abbreviation*

	MORNING PRAYER		60 DAY
DATE	FIRST LESSON	SECOND LESSON	PSALTER—MP
1	Gen 31 † 1-3,17-45	John 16:16-end	78:41-73ᵛ
2 *Presentation*	Gen 32 † 1-13,21-32	Luke 2:22-40	24, 81
3	Gen 33	John 17	83
4	Gen 34	John 18:1-27	86, 87
5	Gen 35	John 18:28-*end*	89:1-18ᵛ
6	Gen 36 † 1-8	John 19:1-37	90
7	Gen 37 † 3-8,12-36	John 19:38-*end*	92, 93
8	Gen 38 † 1-26	John 20	95, 96
9	Gen 39	John 21	99, 100, 101
10	Gen 40	Matt 1:1-17	103
11	Gen 41 † 1-15,25-40	Matt 1:18-*end*	105:1-22ᵛ
12	Gen 42 † 1-28	Matt 2	106:1-18ᵛ
13	Gen 43 † 1-10,15-34	Matt 3	107:1-22
14	Gen 44 † 1-20,30-34	Matt 4	108, 110
15	Gen 45	Matt 5:1-20	111, 112
16	Gen 46 † 1-7,28-34	Matt 5:21-*end*	115
17	Gen 47 † 1-15,23-31	Matt 6:1-18	119:1-24
18	Gen 48	Matt 6:19-*end*	119:49-72
19	Gen 49	Matt 7	119:89-104
20	Gen 50	Matt 8:1-17	119:129-152
21	Exod 1	Matt 8:18-*end*	118
22	Exod 2	Matt 9:1-17	122, 123
23	Exod 3	Matt 9:18-34	127, 128
24 *Matthias*	Acts 1:15-26	Matt 9:35—10:23	132, 133
25	Exod 4	Matt 10:24-*end*	136
26	Exod 5	Matt 11	139
27	Exod 6 † 1-13	Matt 12:1-21	140
28	Exod 7	Matt 12:22-*end*	144

If the year is a leap year, the following lessons are appointed for February 29ᵗʰ:

29	2 Kings 2	Luke 24:44-53	90

‡ *Ash Wednesday falls between February 4ᵗʰ and March 10ᵗʰ. See pages 713-715 to determine its date in a given year. The Lessons are:*

Psalms	First Lesson	Second Lesson	Psalms	First Lesson	Second Lesson
38	Isa 58:1-12	Luke 18:9-14	6, 32	Jonah 3	1 Cor 9:24-27

60 DAY PSALTER—EP	EVENING PRAYER		
	DATE	FIRST LESSON	SECOND LESSON
80	**1**	Jer 31 † 1-17,27-37	1 Cor 15:1-34
84	**2** *Presentation*	Jer 32 † 1-15,36-44	1 Cor 15:35-*end*
85	**3**	Jer 33	1 Cor 16
88	**4**	Jer 34	2 Cor 1:1—2:11
89:19-51ᵛ	**5**	Jer 35	2 Cor 2:12—3 *end*
91	**6**	Jer 36 † 1-10,19-32	2 Cor 4
94	**7**	Jer 37	2 Cor 5
97, 98	**8**	Jer 38	2 Cor 6
102	**9**	Jer 39	2 Cor 7
104	**10**	Jer 40	2 Cor 8
105:23-44ᵛ	**11**	Jer 41	2 Cor 9
106:19-46ᵛ	**12**	Jer 42	2 Cor 10
107:23-43	**13**	Jer 43	2 Cor 11
109	**14**	Jer 44 † 1-19,24-30	2 Cor 12:1-13
113, 114	**15**	Jer 45	2 Cor 12:14—13 *end*
116, 117	**16**	Jer 46	Rom 1
119:25-48	**17**	Jer 47	Rom 2
119:73-88	**18**	Jer 48 † 1-20,40-47	Rom 3
119:105-128	**19**	Jer 49 † 1-13,23-39	Rom 4
119:153-176	**20**	Jer 50 † 1-20,33-40	Rom 5
120, 121	**21**	Jer 51 † 6-10,45-64	Rom 6
124, 125, 126	**22**	Jer 52 † 1-27,31-34	Rom 7
129, 130, 131	**23**	*Baruch* 4 † 5-13,21-37	Rom 8:1-17
134, 135	**24** *Matthias*	*Baruch* 5	Rom 8:18-*end*
137, 138	**25**	Lam 1 † 1-12,17-22	Rom 9
141, 142	**26**	Lam 2 † 1-18	Rom 10
143	**27**	Lam 3 † 1-9,19-33,52-66	Rom 11
145	**28**	Lam 4	Rom 12

104	**29**	Joel 2 † 1-2,12-32	2 Pet 3

† *Optional abbreviation*

	MORNING PRAYER		60 DAY
DATE	FIRST LESSON	SECOND LESSON	PSALTER—MP
1	Exod 8	Matt 13:1-23	146
2	Exod 9 †1-29,33-34	Matt 13:24-43	148
3	Exod 10	Matt 13:44-end	1, 2
4	Exod 11	Matt 14	5, 6
5	Exod 12 †1-20,28-36	Matt 15:1-28	9
6	Exod 13	Matt 15:29—16:12	8, 11
7	Exod 14 †5-31	Matt 16:13-end	12, 13, 14
8	Exod 15	Matt 17:1-23	18:1-20ᵛ
9	Exod 16 †1-7,11-33	Matt 17:24—18:14	19
10	Exod 17	Matt 18:15-end	22
11	Exod 18	Matt 19:1-15	25
12	Exod 19	Matt 19:16—20:16	26, 28
13	Exod 20	Matt 20:17-end	29, 30
14	Exod 21 †1-19,22-29	Matt 21:1-22	34
15	Exod 22	Matt 21:23-end	32, 36
16	Exod 23 †1-13,18-30	Matt 22:1-33	37:1-17ᵛ
17	Exod 24	Matt 22:34—23:12	40
18	Exod 25 †1-23,31-40	Matt 23:13-end	42, 43
19 *Joseph*	Exod 26 †1-10,15-16,29-37	Matt 24:1-28	45
20	Exod 27	Matt 24:29-end	47, 48
21	Exod 28 †1-6,15-21, 29-43	Matt 25:1-30	50
22	Exod 29 †1-18,35-46	Matt 25:31-end	52, 53, 54
23	Exod 30 †1-3,7-33	Matt 26:1-30	56, 57
24	Exod 31	Matt 26:31-56	59
25 *Annun.*	Exod 32 †1-29	Luke 1:26-38	113, 138
26	Exod 33	Matt 26:57-end	61, 62
27	Exod 34 †1-17,27-35	Matt 27:1-26	68:1-18
28	Exod 35 †1-10,20-35	Matt 27:27-56	69:1-18ᵛ
29	Exod 36 †1-10,18-20, 31-38	Matt 27:57—28 end	66
30	Exod 37 †1-11,16-29	Mark 1:1-13	71
31	Exod 38 †1-23	Mark 1:14-31	74

† *Optional abbreviation*

‡ *See page 744 for proper lessons for Maundy Thursday through Easter Day*

60 DAY PSALTER—EP	EVENING PRAYER		
	DATE	FIRST LESSON	SECOND LESSON
147	1	Lam 5	Rom 13
149, 150	2	Prov 1	Rom 14
3, 4	3	Prov 2	Rom 15
7	4	Prov 3 † 1-27	Rom 16
10	5	Prov 4	Phil 1:1-11
15, 16	6	Prov 5	Phil 1:12-*end*
17	7	Prov 6 † 1-11,20-35	Phil 2:1-11
18:21-52ᵛ	8	Prov 7	Phil 2:12-*end*
20, 21	9	Prov 8	Phil 3
23, 24	10	Prov 9	Phil 4
27	11	Prov 10	Col 1:1-20
31	12	Prov 11	Col 1:21—2:7
33	13	Prov 12	Col 2:8-19
35	14	Prov 13	Col 2:20—3:11
38	15	Prov 14	Col 3:12-*end*
37:18-41ᵛ	16	Prov 15	Col 4
39, 41	17	Prov 16	Philemon
44	18	Prov 17	Eph 1:1-14
46	19 *Joseph*	Eph 1:15-*end*	Matt 1:18-*end*
49	20	Prov 18	Eph 2:1-10
51	21	Prov 19	Eph 2:11-*end*
55	22	Prov 20	Eph 3
58, 60	23	Prov 21	Eph 4:1-16
63, 64	24	Prov 22	Eph 4:17-*end*
131, 132	25 *Annun.*	Prov 23	Eph 5:1-17
65, 67	26	Prov 24 † 1-14, 23-34	Eph 5:18-*end*
68:19-36ᵛ	27	Prov 25	Eph 6:1-9
69:19-37ᵛ	28	Prov 26	Eph 6:10-*end*
70, 72	29	Prov 27	1 Tim 1:1-17
73	30	Prov 28	1 Tim 1:18—2 *end*
77	31	Prov 29	1 Tim 3

† *Optional abbreviation*

MAUNDY THURSDAY *through*
EASTER DAY

Maundy Thursday falls between March 19th and April 22nd. See pages 713-715 to determine its date in a given year. The readings for it, and through Easter Day, replace those appointed for the Calendar dates.

	Psalms	First Lesson	Second Lesson	Psalms	First Lesson	Second Lesson
MAUNDY THURSDAY	41	Dan 9	John 13:1-20	142, 143	1 Cor 10:1-22	John 13:21-38
GOOD FRIDAY	40	Lam 3:1-36	John 18	102	1 Pet 2:11-25	Luke 23:18-49
HOLY SATURDAY	88	Lam 3:37-58	Heb 4	91	1 Pet 4:1-8	Luke 23:50-56
EASTER DAY	118	Exod 15	Acts 2:22-32	111,113,114	Rom 6	Luke 24:13-43

Ascension falls between April 30th and June 3rd. See pages 713-715 to determine its date in a given year. The readings are:

	Psalms	First Lesson	Second Lesson	Psalms	First Lesson	Second Lesson
ASCENSION	8, 47	2 Kings 2	Eph 4:1-17	21, 24	Heb 8	Luke 24:44-53

Pentecost falls between May 10th and June 13th. See pages 713-715 to determine its date in a given year. The readings are:

	Psalms	First Lesson	Second Lesson	Psalms	First Lesson	Second Lesson
PENTECOST	48	Isa 11	John 16:1-15	145	Acts 2	Acts 10:34-end

APRIL (1)

MORNING PRAYER				60 DAY PSALTER—MP
DATE	FIRST LESSON		SECOND LESSON	
1	Exod 39	† 1-14,27-43	Mark 1:32-*end*	75, 76
2	Exod 40	† 1-2,16-38	Mark 2:1-22	78:1-18[v]
3	Lev 1		Mark 2:23—3:12	78:41-73[v]
4	Lev 8	† 1-24,30-36	Mark 3:13-*end*	81
5	Lev 10		Mark 4:1-34	84
6	Lev 16	† 1-22,29-34	Mark 4:35—5:20	86, 87
7	Lev 17		Mark 5:21-*end*	89:1-18[v]
8	Lev 18		Mark 6:1-29	90
9	Lev 19	† 1-2,9-37	Mark 6:30-*end*	92, 93
10	Lev 20		Mark 7:1-23	95, 96
11	Lev 23	† 9-32,39-43	Mark 7:24—8:10	99, 100, 101
12	Lev 26	† 3-20,38-46	Mark 8:11-*end*	103
13	Num 6		Mark 9:1-29	105:1-22[v]
14	Num 8	† 5-26	Mark 9:30-*end*	106:1-18[v]
15	Num 11	† 4-6,10-33	Mark 10:1-31	107:1-22
16	Num 12		Mark 10:32-*end*	108, 110
17	Num 13	† 1-3,17-33	Mark 11:1-26	111, 112
18	Num 14	† 1-31	Mark 11:27—12:12	115
19	Num 15	† 22-41	Mark 12:13-34	119:1-24
20	Num 16	† 1-11,20-38	Mark 12:35—13:13	119:49-72
21	Num 17		Mark 13:14-*end*	119:89-104
22	Num 18	† 1-24	Mark 14:1-25	119:129-152
23	Num 20		Mark 14:26-52	118
24	Num 21	† 4-9,21-35	Mark 14:53-*end*	122, 123
25 *Mark*	Acts 12:11-25		Mark 15	127, 128
26	Num 22	† 1-35	Mark 16	132, 133
27	Num 23	† 1-26	Luke 1:1-23	136
28	Num 24		Luke 1:24-56	139
29	Num 25		Luke 1:57-*end*	140
‡ 30	Deut 1	† 1-21,26-33	Luke 2:1-21	144

† *Optional abbreviation*

‡ *See page 745 for proper lessons for Ascension and Pentecost*

60 DAY PSALTER—EP	EVENING PRAYER		
	DATE	FIRST LESSON	SECOND LESSON
79, 82	1	Prov 30 † 1-9,15-33	1 Tim 4
78:19-40ᵛ	2	Prov 31	1 Tim 5
80	3	Job 1	1 Tim 6
83	4	Job 2	Titus 1
85	5	Job 3	Titus 2
88	6	Job 4	Titus 3
89:19-51ᵛ	7	Job 5	2 Tim 1
91	8	Job 6	2 Tim 2
94	9	Job 7	2 Tim 3
97, 98	10	Job 8	2 Tim 4
102	11	Job 9	Heb 1
104	12	Job 10	Heb 2
105:23-44ᵛ	13	Job 11	Heb 3
106:19-46ᵛ	14	Job 12	Heb 4:1-13
107:23-43	15	Job 13	Heb 4:14—5:10
109	16	Job 14	Heb 5:11—6 end
113, 114	17	Job 15	Heb 7
116, 117	18	Job 16	Heb 8
119:25-48	19	Job 17	Heb 9:1-14
119:73-88	20	Job 18	Heb 9:15-end
119:105-128	21	Job 19	Heb 10:1-18
119:153-176	22	Job 20	Heb 10:19-end
120, 121	23	Job 21	Heb 11
124, 125, 126	24	Job 22	Heb 12:1-17
129, 130, 131	25 Mark	Job 23	Heb 12:18-end
134, 135	26	Job 24	Heb 13
137, 138	27	Job 25 & 26	James 1
141, 142	28	Job 27	James 2:1-13
143	29	Job 28	James 2:14-end
145	30	Job 29	James 3

† Optional abbreviation

MORNING PRAYER			60 DAY PSALTER—MP
DATE	FIRST LESSON	SECOND LESSON	
1 *Phil. & Jam.*	Deut 2 † 1-9,14-19,24-37	Luke 2:22-*end*	146
2	Deut 3	Luke 3:1-22	148
3	Deut 4 † 1-18,24-40	Luke 3:23-*end*	1, 2
4	Deut 5	Luke 4:1-30	5, 6
5	Deut 6	Luke 4:31-*end*	9
6	Deut 7	Luke 5:1-16	8, 11
7	Deut 8	Luke 5:17-*end*	12, 13, 14
8	Deut 9	Luke 6:1-19	18:1-20^v
9	Deut 10	Luke 6:20-38	19
10	Deut 11	Luke 6:39—7:10	22
11	Deut 12	Luke 7:11-35	25
12	Deut 13	Luke 7:36-*end*	26, 28
13	Deut 14	Luke 8:1-21	29, 30
14	Deut 15	Luke 8:22-*end*	34
15	Deut 16	Luke 9:1-17	32, 36
16	Deut 17	Luke 9:18-50	37:1-17^v
17	Deut 18	Luke 9:51-*end*	40
18	Deut 19	Luke 10:1-24	42, 43
19	Deut 20	Luke 10:25-*end*	45
20	Deut 21	Luke 11:1-28	47, 48
21	Deut 22	Luke 11:29-*end*	50
22	Deut 23	Luke 12:1-34	52, 53, 54
23	Deut 24	Luke 12:35-53	56, 57
24	Deut 25	Luke 12:54—13:9	59
25	Deut 26	Luke 13:10-*end*	61, 62
26	Deut 27	Luke 14:1-24	68:1-18
27	Deut 28 † 1-25,64-68	Luke 14:25—15:10	69:1-18^v
28	Deut 29	Luke 15:11-*end*	66
29	Deut 30	Luke 16	71
30	Deut 31	Luke 17:1-19	74
31 *Visitation*	Deut 32 † 1-10,15-22,39-52	Luke 1:39-56	75, 76

† *Optional abbreviation*

60 DAY PSALTER—EP	EVENING PRAYER		
	DATE	FIRST LESSON	SECOND LESSON
147	1 *Phil. & Jam.*	James 4	John 1:43-*end*
149, 150	2	Job 30	James 5
3, 4	3	Job 31 † 1-23,35-40	1 Pet 1:1-21
7	4	Job 32	1 Pet 1:22—2:10
10	5	Job 33	1 Pet 2:11—3:7
15, 16	6	Job 34 † 1-15,21-28,31-37	1 Pet 3:8—4:6
17	7	Job 35	1 Pet 4:7-*end*
18:21-52ᵛ	8	Job 36	1 Pet 5
20, 21	9	Job 37	2 Pet 1
23, 24	10	Job 38 † 1-27,31-33	2 Pet 2
27	11	Job 39	2 Pet 3
31	12	Job 40	Jude
33	13	Job 41	1 John 1:1—2:6
35	14	Job 42	1 John 2:7-*end*
38	15	Eccl 1	1 John 3:1-10
37:18-41ᵛ	16	Eccl 2	1 John 3:11—4:6
39, 41	17	Eccl 3	1 John 4:7-*end*
44	18	Eccl 4	1 John 5
46	19	Eccl 5	2 John
49	20	Eccl 6	3 John
51	21	Eccl 7	Acts 1:1-14
55	22	Eccl 8	Acts 1:15-*end*
58, 60	23	Eccl 9	Acts 2:1-21
63, 64	24	Eccl 10	Acts 2:22-*end*
65, 67	25	Eccl 11	Acts 3:1—4:4
68:19-36ᵛ	26	Eccl 12	Acts 4:5-31
69:19-37ᵛ	27	Ezek 1	Acts 4:32—5:11
70, 72	28	Ezek 2	Acts 5:12-*end*
73	29	Ezek 3	Acts 6:1—7:16
77	30	Ezek 4	Acts 7:17-34
79, 82	31 *Visitation*	Ezek 5	Acts 7:35—8:3

† *Optional abbreviation*

	MORNING PRAYER		60 DAY PSALTER—MP
DATE	FIRST LESSON	SECOND LESSON	
1	Deut 33	Luke 17:20-*end*	78:1-18ᵛ
2	Deut 34	Luke 18:1-30	78:41-73ᵛ
3	Josh 1	Luke 18:31—19:10	81
4	Josh 2	Luke 19:11-28	84
5	Josh 3	Luke 19:29-*end*	86, 87
6	Josh 4	Luke 20:1-26	89:1-18ᵛ
7	Josh 5	Luke 20:27—21:4	90
8	Josh 6	Luke 21:5-*end*	92, 93
9	Josh 7	Luke 22:1-38	95, 96
10	Josh 8 † 1-22,30-35	Luke 22:39-53	99, 100, 101
11 *Barnabas*	Acts 4:32-37	Luke 22:54-*end*	103
12	Josh 9	Luke 23:1-25	105:1-22ᵛ
13	Josh 10 † 1-27,40-43	Luke 23:26-49	106:1-18ᵛ
14	Josh 14 † 5-15	Luke 23:50—24:12	107:1-22
15	Josh 22 † 7-31	Luke 24:13-*end*	108, 110
16	Josh 23	Gal 1	111, 112
17	Josh 24 † 1-31	Gal 2	115
18	Judg 1 † 1-21	Gal 3	119:1-24
19	Judg 2 † 6-23	Gal 4	119:49-72
20	Judg 3 † 7-30	Gal 5	119:89-104
21	Judg 4	Gal 6	119:129-152
22	Judg 5 † 1-5,19-31	1 Thess 1	118
23	Judg 6 † 1,6,11-24,33-40	1 Thess 2:1-16	122, 123
24 *Nat. Bap.*	1 Thess 2:17—3 *end*	Matt 14:1-13	127, 128
25	Judg 7 † 1-8,16-25	1 Thess 4:1-12	132, 133
26	Judg 8 † 4-23,28	1 Thess 4:13—5:11	136
27	Judg 9 † 1-6,22-25,43-56	1 Thess 5:12-*end*	139
28	Judg 10 † 6-18	2 Thess 1	140
29 *Pet. & Paul*	2 Thess 2	2 Pet 3:14-*end*	144
30	Judg 11 † 1-11,29-40	2 Thess 3	146

† *Optional abbreviation*

60 DAY PSALTER–EP	EVENING PRAYER		
	DATE	FIRST LESSON	SECOND LESSON
78:19-40ᵛ	**1**	Ezek 6	Acts 8:4-25
80	**2**	Ezek 7	Acts 8:26-*end*
83	**3**	Ezek 8	Acts 9:1-31
85	**4**	Ezek 9	Acts 9:32-*end*
88	**5**	Ezek 10	Acts 10:1-23
89:19-51ᵛ	**6**	Ezek 11	Acts 10:24-*end*
91	**7**	Ezek 12	Acts 11:1-18
94	**8**	Ezek 13	Acts 11:19-*end*
97, 98	**9**	Ezek 14	Acts 12:1-24
102	**10**	Ezek 15	Acts 12:25—13:12
104	**11** *Barnabas*	Ezek 16 † 1-15,33-47,59-63	Acts 13:13-43
105:23-44ᵛ	**12**	Ezek 17	Acts 13:44—14:7
106:19-46ᵛ	**13**	Ezek 18	Acts 14:8-*end*
107:23-43	**14**	Ezek 33 † 1-23,30-33	Acts 15:1-21
109	**15**	Ezek 34	Acts 15:22-35
113, 114	**16**	Ezek 35	Acts 15:36—16:5
116, 117	**17**	Ezek 36 † 16-37	Acts 16:6-*end*
119:25-48	**18**	Ezek 37	Acts 17:1-15
119:73-88	**19**	Ezek 40 † 1-5,17-19,35-49	Acts 17:16-*end*
119:105-128	**20**	Ezek 43	Acts 18:1-23
119:153-176	**21**	Ezek 47	Acts 18:24—19:7
120, 121	**22**	Dan 1	Acts 19:8-20
124, 125, 126	**23**	Dan 2 † 1-14,25-28,31-45	Acts 19:21-*end*
129, 130, 131	**24** *Nat. Bap.*	Dan 3	Acts 20:1-16
134, 135	**25**	Dan 4 † 1-9,19-35	Acts 20:17-*end*
137, 138	**26**	Dan 5	Acts 21:1-16
141, 142	**27**	Dan 6	Acts 21:17-36
143	**28**	Dan 7	Acts 21:37—22:22
145	**29** *Pet. & Paul*	Dan 8	Acts 22:23—23:11
147	**30**	Dan 9	Acts 23:12-*end*

† *Optional abbreviation*

	MORNING PRAYER		60 DAY PSALTER—MP
DATE	FIRST LESSON	SECOND LESSON	
1	Judg 12	1 Cor 1:1-25	148
2	Judg 13	1 Cor 1:26—2 end	1, 2
3	Judg 14	1 Cor 3	5, 6
4	Judg 15	1 Cor 4:1-17	9
5	Judg 16	1 Cor 4:18—5 end	8, 11
6	Ruth 1	1 Cor 6	12, 13, 14
7	Ruth 2	1 Cor 7	18:1-20ᵛ
8	Ruth 3	1 Cor 8	19
9	Ruth 4	1 Cor 9	22
10	1 Sam 1 † 1-20	1 Cor 10	25
11	1 Sam 2 † 1-21	1 Cor 11	26, 28
12	1 Sam 3	1 Cor 12	29, 30
13	1 Sam 4	1 Cor 13	34
14	1 Sam 5	1 Cor 14:1-19	32, 36
15	1 Sam 6 † 1-15	1 Cor 14:20-end	37:1-17ᵛ
16	1 Sam 7	1 Cor 15:1-34	40
17	1 Sam 8	1 Cor 15:35-end	42, 43
18	1 Sam 9	1 Cor 16	45
19	1 Sam 10	2 Cor 1:1—2:11	47, 48
20	1 Sam 11	2 Cor 2:12—3 end	50
21	1 Sam 12	2 Cor 4	52, 53, 54
22 Mary Mag.	2 Cor 5	Luke 7:36—8:3	56, 57
23	1 Sam 13	2 Cor 6	59
24	1 Sam 14 † 1-15,20,24-30	2 Cor 7	61, 62
25 James	2 Cor 8	Mark 1:14-20	68:1-18
26	1 Sam 15	2 Cor 9	69:1-18ᵛ
27	1 Sam 16	2 Cor 10	66
28	1 Sam 17 † 1-11,26-27,31-51	2 Cor 11	71
29	1 Sam 18	2 Cor 12:1-13	74
30	1 Sam 19	2 Cor 12:14—13 end	75, 76
31	1 Sam 20 † 1-7,24-42	Rom 1	78:1-18ᵛ

† *Optional abbreviation*

60 DAY PSALTER—EP	EVENING PRAYER		
	DATE	FIRST LESSON	SECOND LESSON
149, 150	1	Dan 10	Acts 24:1-23
3, 4	2	Dan 11 † 1-19	Acts 24:24—25:12
7	3	Dan 12	Acts 25:13-*end*
10	4	*Susanna*	Acts 26
15, 16	5	Esth 1	Acts 27
17	6	Esth 2	Acts 28:1-15
18:21-52ᵛ	7	Esth 3	Acts 28:16-*end*
20, 21	8	Esth 4	Philemon
23, 24	9	Esth 5	1 Tim 1:1-17
27	10	Esth 6	1 Tim 1:18—2 *end*
31	11	Esth 7	1 Tim 3
33	12	Esth 8	1 Tim 4
35	13	Esth 9 & 10	1 Tim 5
38	14	Ezra 1	1 Tim 6
37:18-41ᵛ	15	Ezra 3	Titus 1
39, 41	16	Ezra 4	Titus 2
44	17	Ezra 5	Titus 3
46	18	Ezra 6	2 Tim 1
49	19	Ezra 7	2 Tim 2
51	20	Ezra 8 † 21-36	2 Tim 3
55	21	Ezra 9	2 Tim 4
58, 60	22 *Mary Mag.*	Ezra 10 † 1-16	John 1:1-28
63, 64	23	Neh 1	John 1:29-*end*
65, 67	24	Neh 2	John 2
68:19-36ᵛ	25 *James*	Neh 3 † 1-15	John 3:1-21
69:19-37ᵛ	26	Neh 4	John 3:22-*end*
70, 72	27	Neh 5	John 4:1-26
73	28	Neh 6	John 4:27-*end*
77	29	Neh 8	John 5:1-24
79, 82	30	Neh 9 † 1-15,26-38	John 5:25-*end*
78:19-40ᵛ	31	Neh 10 † 28-39	John 6:1-21

† *Optional abbreviation*

	MORNING PRAYER		60 DAY
DATE	FIRST LESSON	SECOND LESSON	PSALTER—MP
1	1 Sam 21	Rom 2	78:41-73ᵛ
2	1 Sam 22	Rom 3	81
3	1 Sam 23	Rom 4	84
4	1 Sam 24	Rom 5	86, 87
5	1 Sam 25 † 1-19,23-25,32-42	Rom 6	89:1-18ᵛ
6 *Transfig.*	Rom 7	Mark 9:2-10	27
7	1 Sam 26	Rom 8:1-17	90
8	1 Sam 27	Rom 8:18-*end*	92, 93
9	1 Sam 28	Rom 9	95, 96
10	1 Sam 29	Rom 10	99, 100, 101
11	1 Sam 30 † 1-25	Rom 11	103
12	1 Sam 31	Rom 12	105:1-22ᵛ
13	2 Sam 1	Rom 13	106:1-18ᵛ
14	2 Sam 2 † 1-17,26-31	Rom 14	107:1-22
15 *Mary Virg.*	2 Sam 3 † 6-11,17-39	Luke 1:26-38	108, 110
16	2 Sam 4	Rom 15	111, 112
17	2 Sam 5	Rom 16	115
18	2 Sam 6	Phil 1:1-11	119:1-24
19	2 Sam 7	Phil 1:12-*end*	119:49-72
20	2 Sam 8	Phil 2:1-11	119:89-104
21	2 Sam 9	Phil 2:12-*end*	119:129-152
22	2 Sam 10	Phil 3	118
23	2 Sam 11	Phil 4	122, 123
24 *Bart.*	Col 1:1-20	Luke 6:12-16	127, 128
25	2 Sam 12 † 1-25	Col 1:21—2:7	132, 133
26	2 Sam 13 † 1-29,38-39	Col 2:8-19	136
27	2 Sam 14 † 1-21,28	Col 2:20—3:11	139
28	2 Sam 15 † 1-18,23-25,32-34	Col 3:12-*end*	140
29	2 Sam 16	Col 4	144
30	2 Sam 17 † 1-23	Philemon	146
31	2 Sam 18 † 1-15,19-33	Eph 1:1-14	148

† *Optional abbreviation*

60 DAY PSALTER–EP	EVENING PRAYER		
	DATE	FIRST LESSON	SECOND LESSON
80	1	Neh 12 † 27-47	John 6:22-40
83	2	Neh 13 † 1-22,30-31	John 6:41-end
85	3	Hos 1	John 7:1-24
88	4	Hos 2	John 7:25-52
89:19-51ᵛ	5	Hos 3	John 7:53—8:30
80	6 Transfig.	Hos 4	John 8:31-end
91	7	Hos 5	John 9
94	8	Hos 6	John 10:1-21
97, 98	9	Hos 7	John 10:22-end
102	10	Hos 8	John 11:1-44
104	11	Hos 9	John 11:45-end
105:23-44ᵛ	12	Hos 10	John 12:1-19
106:19-46ᵛ	13	Hos 11	John 12:20-end
107:23-43	14	Hos 12	John 13
109	15 Mary Virg.	Hos 13	John 14:1-14
113, 114	16	Hos 14	John 14:15-end
116, 117	17	Joel 1	John 15:1-17
119:25-48	18	Joel 2 † 1-17,28-32	John 15:18-end
119:73-88	19	Joel 3	John 16:1-15
119:105-128	20	Amos 1	John 16:16-end
119:153-176	21	Amos 2	John 17
120, 121	22	Amos 3	John 18:1-27
124, 125, 126	23	Amos 4	John 18:28-end
129, 130, 131	24 Bart.	Amos 5	John 19:1-37
134, 135	25	Amos 6	John 19:38-end
137, 138	26	Amos 7	John 20
141, 142	27	Amos 8	John 21
143	28	Amos 9	Matt 1:1-17
145	29	Obadiah	Matt 1:18-end
147	30	Jonah 1	Matt 2
149, 150	31	Jonah 2	Matt 3

† *Optional abbreviation*

	MORNING PRAYER		60 DAY PSALTER—MP
DATE	FIRST LESSON	SECOND LESSON	
1	2 Sam 19 † 1-30	Eph 1:15-*end*	1, 2
2	2 Sam 20	Eph 2:1-10	5, 6
3	2 Sam 21	Eph 2:11-*end*	9
4	2 Sam 22 † 1-7,14-20,32-51	Eph 3	8, 11
5	2 Sam 23 † 1-23	Eph 4:1-16	12, 13, 14
6	2 Sam 24	Eph 4:17-*end*	18:1-20ᵛ
7	1 Chron 22	Eph 5:1-17	19
8	1 Kings 1 † 1-18,29-40	Eph 5:18-*end*	22
9	1 Chron 28	Eph 6	25
10	1 Kings 2 † 1-25	Heb 1	26, 28
11	1 Kings 3	Heb 2	29, 30
12	1 Kings 4 † 1-6,20-34	Heb 3	34
13	1 Kings 5	Heb 4:1-13	32, 36
14 *Holy Cross*	Heb 4:14—5:10	John 12:23-33	37:1-17ᵛ
15	1 Kings 6 † 1-7,11-30,37-38	Heb 5:11—6 *end*	40
16	1 Kings 7 † 1-14,40-44,47-51	Heb 7	42, 43
17	1 Kings 8 † 1-11,22-30,54-63	Heb 8	45
18	1 Kings 9 † 1-9,15-28	Heb 9:1-14	47, 48
19	1 Kings 10 †1-13,23-29	Heb 9:15-*end*	50
20	1 Kings 11 † 1-14,23-33,41-43	Heb 10:1-18	52, 53, 54
21 *Matthew*	Heb 10:19-*end*	Matt 9:9-13	56, 57
22	1 Kings 12 † 1-20,25-30	Heb 11	59
23	1 Kings 13 † 1-25,33-34	Heb 12:1-17	61, 62
24	1 Kings 14	Heb 12:18-*end*	68:1-18
25	2 Chron 12	Heb 13	69:1-18ᵛ
26	2 Chron 13	James 1	66
27	2 Chron 14	James 2:1-13	71
28	2 Chron 15	James 2:14-*end*	74
29 *Michael*	Rev 12:7-12	James 3	75, 76
30	2 Chron 16	James 4	78:1-18ᵛ

† *Optional abbreviation*

60 DAY PSALTER—EP	\multicolumn{4}{c}{EVENING PRAYER}
	DATE	FIRST LESSON	SECOND LESSON
3, 4	1	Jonah 3	Matt 4
7	2	Jonah 4	Matt 5:1-20
10	3	Mic 1	Matt 5:21-*end*
15, 16	4	Mic 2	Matt 6:1-18
17	5	Mic 3	Matt 6:19-*end*
18:21-52ᵛ	6	Mic 4	Matt 7
20, 21	7	Mic 5	Matt 8:1-17
23, 24	8	Mic 6	Matt 8:18-*end*
27	9	Mic 7	Matt 9:1-17
31	10	Nahum 1	Matt 9:18-34
33	11	Nahum 2	Matt 9:35—10:23
35	12	Nahum 3	Matt 10:24-*end*
38	13	Hab 1	Matt 11
37:18-41ᵛ	14 *Holy Cross*	Hab 2	Matt 12:1-21
39, 41	15	Hab 3	Matt 12:22-*end*
44	16	Zeph 1	Matt 13:1-23
46	17	Zeph 2	Matt 13:24-43
49	18	Zeph 3	Matt 13:44-*end*
51	19	Hag 1	Matt 14
55	20	Hag 2	Matt 15:1-28
58, 60	21 *Matthew*	Zech 1	Matt 15:29—16:12
63, 64	22	Zech 2	Matt 16:13-*end*
65, 67	23	Zech 3	Matt 17:1-23
68:19-36ᵛ	24	Zech 4	Matt 17:24—18:14
69:19-37ᵛ	25	Zech 5	Matt 18:15-*end*
70, 72	26	Zech 6	Matt 19:1-15
73	27	Zech 7	Matt 19:16—20:16
77	28	Zech 8	Matt 20:17-*end*
79, 82	29 *Michael*	Zech 9	Matt 21:1-22
78:19-40ᵛ	30	Zech 10	Matt 21:23-*end*

† *Optional abbreviation*

	MORNING PRAYER		60 DAY
DATE	FIRST LESSON	SECOND LESSON	PSALTER—MP
1	1 Kings 15 † 1-30	James 5	78:41-73ᵛ
2	1 Kings 16 † 1-4,8-19,23-34	1 Pet 1:1-21	81
3	1 Kings 17	1 Pet 1:22—2:10	84
4	1 Kings 18 † 1-8,17-46	1 Pet 2:11—3:7	86,87
5	1 Kings 19	1 Pet 3:8—4:6	89:1-18ᵛ
6	1 Kings 20 † 1,13,21-43	1 Pet 4:7-*end*	90
7	1 Kings 21	1 Pet 5	92,93
8	1 Kings 22 † 1-23,29-38	2 Pet 1	95,96
9	2 Chron 20	2 Pet 2	99, 100, 101
10	2 Kings 1	2 Pet 3	103
11	2 Kings 2	Jude	105:1-22ᵛ
12	2 Kings 3	1 John 1:1—2:6	106:1-18ᵛ
13	2 Kings 4 † 8-37	1 John 2:7-*end*	107:1-22
14	2 Kings 5	1 John 3:1-10	108, 110
15	2 Kings 6 † 1-24	1 John 3:11—4:6	111, 112
16	2 Kings 7	1 John 4:7-*end*	115
17	2 Kings 8 † 1-19,25-27	1 John 5	119:1-24
18 *Luke*	2 John	Luke 1:1-4	119:49-72
19	2 Kings 9 † 1-26,30-37	3 John	119:89-104
20	2 Kings 10 † 1-11,18-31	Acts 1:1-14	119:129-152
21	2 Kings 11	Acts 1:15-*end*	118
22	2 Kings 12	Acts 2:1-21	122, 123
23 *James Jer.*	Acts 2:22-*end*	James 1	127, 128
24	2 Kings 13	Acts 3:1—4:4	132, 133
25	2 Kings 14	Acts 4:5-31	136
26	2 Chron 26	Acts 4:32—5:11	139
27	2 Kings 15 † 1-29	Acts 5:12-*end*	140
28 *Sim. & Jude*	Acts 6:1—7:16	John 14:15-31	144
29	2 Kings 16	Acts 7:17-34	146
30	2 Kings 17 † 1-28,41	Acts 7:35—8:3	148
31	2 Chron 28	Acts 8:4-25	2

† *Optional abbreviation*

60 DAY PSALTER—EP	EVENING PRAYER		
	DATE	FIRST LESSON	SECOND LESSON
80	1	Zech 11	Matt 22:1-33
83	2	Zech 12	Matt 22:34—23:12
85	3	Zech 13	Matt 23:13-*end*
88	4	Zech 14	Matt 24:1-28
89:19-51ᵛ	5	Mal 1	Matt 24:29-*end*
91	6	Mal 2	Matt 25:1-30
94	7	Mal 3	Matt 25:31-*end*
97, 98	8	Mal 4	Matt 26:1-30
102	9	1 *Macc* 1 † 1-15,20-25,41-64	Matt 26:31-56
104	10	1 *Macc* 2 † 1-28	Matt 26:57-*end*
105:23-44ᵛ	11	2 *Macc* 6	Matt 27:1-26
106:19-46ᵛ	12	2 *Macc* 7	Matt 27:27-56
107:23-43	13	2 *Macc* 8 † 1-29	Matt 27:57—28 *end*
109	14	2 *Macc* 10 † 1-8,24-38	Mark 1:1-13
113, 114	15	1 *Macc* 7 † 1-6,23-50	Mark 1:14-31
116, 117	16	1 *Macc* 9 † 1-31	Mark 1:32-*end*
119:25-48	17	1 *Macc* 13 † 1-30,41-42	Mark 2:1-22
119:73-88	18 *Luke*	1 *Macc* 14 † 4-18,35-43	Mark 2:23—3:12
119:105-128	19	Isa 1	Mark 3:13-*end*
119:153-176	20	Isa 2	Mark 4:1-34
120, 121	21	Isa 3	Mark 4:35—5:20
124, 125, 126	22	Isa 4	Mark 5:21-*end*
129, 130, 131	23 *James Jer.*	Isa 5	Mark 6:1-29
134, 135	24	Isa 6	Mark 6:30-*end*
137, 138	25	Isa 7	Mark 7:1-23
141, 142	26	Isa 8	Mark 7:24—8:10
143	27	Isa 9	Mark 8:11-*end*
145	28 *Sim. & Jude*	Isa 10	Mark 9:1-29
147	29	Isa 11	Mark 9:30-*end*
149, 150	30	Isa 12	Mark 10:1-31
3, 4	31	Isa 13	Mark 10:32-*end*

† *Optional abbreviation*

	MORNING PRAYER		60 DAY PSALTER—MP
DATE	FIRST LESSON	SECOND LESSON	
1 *All Saints'*	Heb 11:32—12:2	Acts 8:26-*end*	1, 15
2	2 Chron 29 † 1-11,20-30,35-36	Acts 9:1-31	5, 6
3	2 Chron 30 † 1-22,26-27	Acts 9:32-*end*	9
4	2 Kings 18 † 1-13,17-30,35-37	Acts 10:1-23	8, 11
5	2 Kings 19 † 1-20,29-31,35-37	Acts 10:24-*end*	12, 13, 14
6	2 Kings 20	Acts 11:1-18	18:1-20ᵛ
7	2 Chron 33	Acts 11:19-*end*	19
8	2 Kings 21	Acts 12:1-24	22
9	2 Kings 22	Acts 12:25—13:12	25
10	2 Kings 23 † 1-20,26-30	Acts 13:13-43	26, 28
11	2 Kings 24	Acts 13:44—14:7	29, 30
12	2 Kings 25 † 1-22,25-30	Acts 14:8-*end*	34
13	*Judith* 4	Acts 15:1-21	32, 36
14	*Judith* 8	Acts 15:22-35	37:1-17ᵛ
15	*Judith* 9	Acts 15:36—16:5	40
16	*Judith* 10	Acts 16:6-*end*	42, 43
17	*Judith* 11	Acts 17:1-15	45
18	*Judith* 12	Acts 17:16-*end*	47, 48
19	*Judith* 13	Acts 18:1-23	50
20	*Judith* 14	Acts 18:24—19:7	52, 53, 54
21	*Judith* 15	Acts 19:8-20	56, 57
22	*Judith* 16	Acts 19:21-*end*	59
23	*Ecclesiasticus* 1	Acts 20:1-16	61, 62
24	*Ecclesiasticus* 2	Acts 20:17-*end*	68:1-18
25	*Ecclesiasticus* 4 † 1-19	Acts 21:1-16	69:1-18ᵛ
26	*Ecclesiasticus* 6 † 5-31	Acts 21:17-36	66
27	*Ecclesiasticus* 7 † 1-21,27-36	Acts 21:37—22:22	71
28	*Ecclesiasticus* 9	Acts 22:23—23:11	74
29	*Ecclesiasticus* 10 † 1-24	Acts 23:12-*end*	75, 76
30 *Andrew*	*Ecclesiasticus* 11 † 1-9,18-28	John 1:35-42	78:1-18ᵛ

† *Optional abbreviation*

60 DAY PSALTER—EP	EVENING PRAYER		
	DATE	FIRST LESSON	SECOND LESSON
34	1 *All Saints'*	Isa 14	Rev 19:1-16
7	2	Isa 15	Mark 11:1-26
10	3	Isa 16	Mark 11:27—12:12
15, 16	4	Isa 17	Mark 12:13-34
17	5	Isa 18	Mark 12:35—13:13
18:21-52ᵛ	6	Isa 19	Mark 13:14-*end*
20, 21	7	Isa 20	Mark 14:1-25
23, 24	8	Isa 21	Mark 14:26-52
27	9	Isa 22	Mark 14:53-*end*
31	10	Isa 23	Mark 15
33	11	Isa 24	Mark 16
35	12	Isa 25	Luke 1:1-23
38	13	Isa 26	Luke 1:24-56
37:18-41ᵛ	14	Isa 27	Luke 1:57-*end*
39, 41	15	Isa 28	Luke 2:1-21
44	16	Isa 29	Luke 2:22-*end*
46	17	Isa 30	Luke 3:1-22
49	18	Isa 31	Luke 3:23-*end*
51	19	Isa 32	Luke 4:1-30
55	20	Isa 33	Luke 4:31-*end*
58, 60	21	Isa 34	Luke 5:1-16
63, 64	22	Isa 35	Luke 5:17-*end*
65, 67	23	Isa 36	Luke 6:1-19
68:19-36ᵛ	24	Isa 37	Luke 6:20-38
69:19-37ᵛ	25	Isa 38	Luke 6:39—7:10
70, 72	26	Isa 39	Luke 7:11-35
73	27	Isa 40	Luke 7:36-*end*
77	28	Isa 41	Luke 8:1-21
79, 82	29	Isa 42	Luke 8:22-*end*
78:19-40ᵛ	30 *Andrew*	Isa 43	Luke 9:1-17

† *Optional abbreviation*

	MORNING PRAYER		60 DAY
DATE	FIRST LESSON	SECOND LESSON	PSALTER—MP
1	*Ecclesiasticus* 14	Acts 24:1-23	78:41-73ᵛ
2	*Ecclesiasticus* 17	Acts 24:24—25:12	81
3	*Ecclesiasticus* 18 † 1-26,30-33	Acts 25:13-*end*	84
4	*Ecclesiasticus* 21	Acts 26	86, 87
5	*Ecclesiasticus* 34	Acts 27	89:1-18ᵛ
6	*Ecclesiasticus* 38 † 1-15,24-34	Acts 28:1-15	90
7	*Ecclesiasticus* 39 † 1-11,16-35	Acts 28:16-*end*	92, 93
8	*Ecclesiasticus* 44	Rev 1	95, 96
9	*Ecclesiasticus* 45	Rev 2:1-17	99, 100, 101
10	*Ecclesiasticus* 46	Rev 2:18—3:6	103
11	*Ecclesiasticus* 47	Rev 3:7-*end*	105:1-22ᵛ
12	*Ecclesiasticus* 48	Rev 4	106:1-18ᵛ
13	*Ecclesiasticus* 49	Rev 5	107:1-22
14	*Ecclesiasticus* 50	Rev 6	108, 110
15	*Ecclesiasticus* 51	Rev 7	111, 112
16	*Wisdom* 1	Rev 8	115
17	*Wisdom* 2	Rev 9	119:1-24
18	*Wisdom* 3	Rev 10	119:49-72
19	*Wisdom* 4	Rev 11	119:89-104
20	*Wisdom* 5	Rev 12	119:129-152
21 *Thomas*	Rev 13	John 14:1-7	118
22	*Wisdom* 6	Rev 14	122, 123
23	*Wisdom* 7	Rev 15	127, 128
24	*Wisdom* 8	Rev 16	132, 133
25 *Christmas*	Isa 9:1-7	Rev 17	19 *or* 45
26 *Stephen*	Acts 6:8—7:6,17-41,44-60	Rev 18	136
27 *John*	Rev 19	John 21:9-25	139
28 *Innocents*	Jer 31:1-17	Rev 20	140
29	*Wisdom* 9	Rev 21:1-14	144
30	*Wisdom* 10	Rev 21:15—22:5	146
31	*Wisdom* 11	Rev 22:6-*end*	148

† *Optional abbreviation*

60 DAY PSALTER—EP		EVENING PRAYER	
	DATE	FIRST LESSON	SECOND LESSON
80	1	Isa 44	Luke 9:18-50
83	2	Isa 45	Luke 9:51-*end*
85	3	Isa 46	Luke 10:1-24
88	4	Isa 47	Luke 10:25-*end*
89:19-51ᵛ	5	Isa 48	Luke 11:1-28
91	6	Isa 49	Luke 11:29-*end*
94	7	Isa 50	Luke 12:1-34
97, 98	8	Isa 51	Luke 12:35-53
102	9	Isa 52	Luke 12:54—13:9
104	10	Isa 53	Luke 13:10-*end*
105:23-44ᵛ	11	Isa 54	Luke 14:1-24
106:19-46ᵛ	12	Isa 55	Luke 14:25—15:10
107:23-43	13	Isa 56	Luke 15:11-*end*
109	14	Isa 57	Luke 16
113, 114	15	Isa 58	Luke 17:1-19
116, 117	16	Isa 59	Luke 17:20-*end*
119:25-48	17	Isa 60	Luke 18:1-30
119:73-88	18	Isa 61	Luke 18:31—19:10
119:105-128	19	Isa 62	Luke 19:11-28
119:153-176	20	Isa 63	Luke 19:29-*end*
120, 121	21 *Thomas*	Isa 64	Luke 20:1-26
124, 125, 126	22	Isa 65	Luke 20:27—21:4
129, 130, 131	23	Isa 66	Luke 21:5-*end*
134, 135	24	Song of Songs 1	Luke 22:1-38
85, 110	25 *Christmas*	Song of Songs 2	Luke 2:1-14
137, 138	26 *Stephen*	Song of Songs 3	Luke 22:39-53
141, 142	27 *John*	Song of Songs 4	Luke 22:54-*end*
143	28 *Innocents*	Song of Songs 5	Luke 23:1-25
145	29	Song of Songs 6	Luke:23:26-49
147	30	Song of Songs 7	Luke 23:50—24:12
149, 150	31	Song of Songs 8	Luke 24:13-*end*

† *Optional abbreviation*

A Selection of

PSALMS

from the

NEW COVERDALE PSALTER

6

Domine, ne in furore

1 O Lord, rebuke me not in your indignation, *
   neither chasten me in your displeasure.
2 Have mercy upon me, O Lord, for I am weak; *
   O Lord, heal me, for my bones are racked.
3 My soul also is greatly troubled; *
   but, Lord, how long will you punish me?
4 Turn, O Lord, and deliver my soul; *
   O save me for your mercy's sake.
5 For in death no one remembers you, *
   and who will give you thanks in the grave?
6 I am weary with my groaning; *
   every night I flood my bed and drench my couch with
   my tears.
7 My eyes have become dim because of trouble, *
   and worn away because of all my enemies.
8 Away from me, all you who work wickedness, *
   for the Lord has heard the voice of my weeping.
9 The Lord has heard my petition; *
   the Lord will receive my prayer.
10 All my enemies shall be confounded and greatly vexed; *
   they shall be turned back and put to shame suddenly.

32

Beati quorum

1 Blessed is the one whose unrighteousness is forgiven, *
　　and whose sin is covered.

2 Blessed is the one to whom the LORD imputes no sin, *
　　and in whose spirit there is no guile.

3 For while I held my tongue, my bones wasted away; *
　　I ceased not from groaning all the day long.

4 For your hand was heavy upon me day and night, *
　　and I was dried up and withered, as in the drought of
　　　summer.

5 Then I acknowledged my sin unto you, *
　　and I did not hide my iniquity.

6 I said, "I will confess my sins unto the LORD"; *
　　and so you forgave the wickedness of my sin.

7 For this reason shall all the godly make their prayers unto you
　　at a time when you may be found; *
　　when the great floodwaters rise, they shall not reach them.

8 You are my hiding-place; you shall preserve me from trouble; *
　　you shall encompass me with songs of deliverance.

9 "I will instruct you and teach you in the way that
　　you should go, *
　　and I will guide you with my eye.

10 Do not be like the horse and mule, which have no
　　understanding, *
　　whose mouths must be held with bit and bridle,
　　or else they will not come near you."

11 Great troubles remain for the ungodly; *
　　but mercy embraces those who trust in the LORD.

12 Be glad, O you righteous, and rejoice in the LORD; *
    and be joyful, all who are true of heart.

38

Domine, ne in furore

1 Rebuke me not, O LORD, in your anger, *
    neither chasten me in your weighty displeasure.
2 For your arrows stick fast in me, *
    and your hand presses me hard.
3 There is no health in my flesh, because of your displeasure; *
    neither is there any rest in my bones, by reason of my sin.
4 For my iniquities have gone over my head *
    and are like a heavy burden, too much for me to bear.
5 My wounds stink and fester, *
    by reason of my foolishness.
6 I am brought into such great trouble and misery *
    that I go about mourning all the day long.
7 For my loins are filled with burning, *
    and there is no wholeness in my body.
8 I am feeble and sorely smitten; *
    I have roared because of the tumult of my heart.
9 Lord, you know all my desire, *
    and my groaning is not hidden from you.
10 My heart is panting, my strength has failed me, *
    and the sight of my eyes is gone from me.
11 My friends and my neighbors turn away from my trouble, *
    and my kinsmen stand afar off.
12 Those also who seek after my life lay snares for me, *
    and those who go about to do me evil talk of wickedness
    and imagine deceit all the day long.

13 As for me, I am like the deaf who do not hear, *
   and as one who is mute, who does not open his mouth.

14 I have become like a man who hears not, *
   and in whose mouth are no reproofs.

15 For in you, O LORD, have I put my trust; *
   you shall answer for me, O Lord my God.

16 I have said, "Let not my enemies triumph over me," *
   for when my foot slipped, they rejoiced greatly over me.

17 Truly, I am about to fall, *
   and my pain is ever with me.

18 For I will confess my wickedness, *
   and be sorry for my sin.

19 But my enemies live, and are mighty, *
   and those who hate me wrongfully are many in number.

20 Those also who repay evil for good are against me, *
   because I follow that which is good.

21 Forsake me not, O LORD my God; *
   O be not far from me.

22 Make haste to help me, *

   O Lord God of my salvation.

51

Miserere mei, Deus

1 Have mercy upon me, O God, in your great goodness; *
   according to the multitude of your mercies wipe away
   my offences.

2 Wash me thoroughly from my wickedness *
   and cleanse me from my sin.

3 For I acknowledge my faults, *
   and my sin is ever before me.

⁴ Against you only have I sinned,
and done this evil in your sight, *
   so that you are justified in your sentence, and blameless
   in your judgment.
⁵ Behold, I was brought forth in wickedness, *
   and in sin my mother conceived me.
⁶ But behold, you desire truth in the inward parts *
   and shall make me understand wisdom secretly.
⁷ You shall purge me with hyssop, and I shall be clean; *
   you shall wash me, and I shall be whiter than snow.
⁸ You shall make me hear of joy and gladness, *
   that the bones which you have broken may rejoice.
⁹ Turn your face from my sins, *
   and blot out all my misdeeds.
¹⁰ Create in me a clean heart, O God, *
   and renew a right spirit within me.
¹¹ Cast me not away from your presence, *
   and take not your holy Spirit from me.
¹² O give me the comfort of your help again, *
   and sustain me with your willing Spirit.
¹³ Then shall I teach your ways unto the wicked, *
   and sinners shall return unto you.
¹⁴ Deliver me from blood-guilt, O God, the God
of my salvation, *
   and my tongue shall sing of your righteousness.
¹⁵ O Lord, open my lips, *
   and my mouth shall show forth your praise.
¹⁶ For you desire no sacrifice, or else I would give it to you; *
   but you delight not in burnt-offerings.

17 The sacrifice of God is a troubled spirit; *
    a broken and contrite heart, O God, you shall not
    despise.
18 O be favorable and gracious unto Zion; *
    may you build up the walls of Jerusalem.
19 Then you shall be pleased with the sacrifice of
righteousness,
with the burnt-offerings and oblations; *
    then shall they offer young bullocks upon your altar.

102

Domine, exaudi

1 Hear my prayer, O Lord, *
    and let my cry come unto you.
2 Hide not your face from me in the time of my trouble; *
    incline your ear to me when I call; O hear me,
    and very soon.
3 For my days are consumed like smoke, *
    and my bones are burnt up as in a furnace.
4 My heart is smitten and withered like grass, *
    so that I forget to eat my bread.
5 Because of the voice of my groaning, *
    my bones will scarcely cleave to my flesh.
6 I have become like an owl in the wilderness *
    and like a screech-owl among the ruins.
7 I am solitary, and lie sleepless because of my groaning; *
    I am like a sparrow that sits alone upon the housetop.
8 My enemies revile me all day long, *
    and those who are enraged against me conspire
    to do me hurt.

9 For I have eaten ashes as if they were bread *
      and mingled my drink with weeping,
10 Because of your indignation and wrath, *
      for you have taken me up and cast me down.
11 My days are gone like a shadow, *
      and I am withered like grass.
12 But you, O Lord, shall endure for ever, *
      and your remembrance throughout all generations.
13 You shall arise and have mercy upon Zion, *
      for it is time for you to have mercy upon her; indeed,
      the time has come.
14 For your servants love her very stones, *
      and are moved to pity to see her in the dust.
15 The nations shall fear your Name, O Lord, *
      and all the kings of the earth your majesty,
16 When the Lord shall build up Zion, *
      and when his glory shall appear,
17 When he turns to the prayer of the destitute *
      and despises not their plea.
18 This shall be written for those that come after, *
      and a people that shall yet be born shall praise the Lord.
19 For he has looked down from his sanctuary; *
      from the heavens the Lord has beheld the earth,
20 That he might hear the groanings of those
    who are in captivity,*
      and deliver those who are condemned to die,
21 That they may declare the Name of the Lord in Zion, *
      and his praises in Jerusalem;
22 When the peoples are gathered together, *
      and the kingdoms also, to serve the Lord.

23 He brought down my strength before my time, *
    and shortened my days.
24 But I said, "O my God, take me not away in the midst of my days; *
    for your years endure throughout all generations."
25 You, Lord, in the beginning laid the foundation of
the earth, *
    and the heavens are the work of your hands.
26 They shall perish, but you shall endure; *
    they all shall wear out, as does a garment;
27 And as a garment you shall change them, and they shall
be changed; *
    but you are the same, and your years shall not fail.
28 The children of your servants shall continue, *
    and their seed shall stand fast in your sight.

130

De profundis

1 Out of the deep have I called unto you, O LORD; *
    Lord, hear my voice.
2 O let your ears consider well *
    the voice of my supplications.
3 If you, LORD, were to mark what is done amiss, *
    O Lord, who could abide it?
4 For there is mercy with you; *
    therefore you shall be feared.
5 I wait for the LORD; my soul waits for him; *
    in his word is my trust.

6 My soul waits for the Lord, *
    more than watchmen for the morning, more than
    watchmen for the morning.
7 O Israel, trust in the Lord, for with the Lord there
  is mercy, *
    and with him is plenteous redemption;
8 And he shall redeem Israel *
    from all their sins.

143

Domine, exaudi

1 Hear my prayer, O Lord, and consider my supplications; *
    hearken to me, for your truth and righteousness' sake.
2 Enter not into judgment with your servant, *
    for in your sight shall no one living be justified.
3 For the enemy has persecuted my soul;
  he has smitten my life down to the ground; *
    he has laid me in the darkness, like those
    who have been long dead.
4 Therefore my spirit faints within me, *
    and my heart within me is desolate.
5 Yet I remember the time past; I muse upon all your works; *
    indeed, I meditate on the works of your hands.
6 I stretch forth my hands to you; *
    my soul gasps for you as a thirsty land.
7 Hear me, O Lord, and very soon, for my spirit grows faint; *
    hide not your face from me, lest I be like those who go
    down into the pit.

8 O let me hear your loving-kindness in the morning,
   for in you have I put my trust; *
      show me the way that I should walk in,
      for I lift up my soul unto you.
9 Deliver me, O Lord, from my enemies, *
   for I flee unto you to hide me.
10 Teach me to do the thing that pleases you,
   for you are my God;*
      let your loving Spirit lead me forth into the land
      of righteousness.
11 Revive me, O Lord, for your Name's sake; *
      and for your righteousness' sake bring my soul out of
      trouble.
12 Of your goodness slay my enemies, *
      and destroy all those who afflict my soul, for I
      am your servant.